PENGUIN BOOKS

THE BOOK OF BOSWELL

Gordon Boswell was born in Blackpool in 1895. His grandfather, 'Wester' Boswell, was the first Gypsy to acquire some formal education, and became known as the grammarian of the ancient Gypsy language; his father, Trafalgar Boswell, was converted by the Gypsy evangelist, John Wesley Baker, and for years ran a mission tent. The family's main business was the raising, training and trading of horses; and after the First World War, during which he served in the Veterinary Corps, Gordon Boswell followed the same life, though he later did a long stint as a scrap merchant. In 1965, when Appleby Fair, the historic meeting-place of English Gypsies, was threatened with closure, he led the deputation that saved it.

Silvester Gordon Boswell

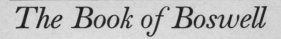

The Book of Boswell

Autobiography of a Gypsy

edited by
John Seymour

PENGUIN BOOKS

Penguin Books Ltd, Harmondsworth, Middlesex, England
Penguin Books Australia Ltd, Ringwood, Victoria, Australia

—

First published by Victor Gollancz 1970
Published in Penguin Books 1973

—

—

Made and printed in Great Britain by
Cox & Wyman Ltd, London, Reading and Fakenham
Set in Linotype Georgian

On the Road Again

It's a long time ago since I was a boy,
I roamed the roads then to and fro,
All towns and hamlets I did know,
From east to west and south to north,
My wagon and horse just travelled on,
To find a lane or common ground,
To rest my horses where good grass could be found,
When this was done, we would find some wood,
And kindle a fire. Oh, Life was good,
The pan and the kettle was on the kettle prop hook,
My dear old mother would start to cook,
The best of everything, now only in a book,
And when it was done she would call us around,
And in no time at all we'd be all sitting down,
And when we had finished we'd lay down to rest,
The sky for our roof, the stars for our light,
Awake in the morning, the lark's on the wing,
The new day has started, we are on the road again,
We will make for the north my father would say,
It's our usual run just this time of the year,
Where trade's at its best, we must go for our share,
The country's at its best, and nature's unspoilt,
It belongs to the Romany, the rich and the poor,
The king was the oak tree, the queen was the ash,
The thrush and the blackbirds to give us their songs,
Life was worth living with all this around,
We would rest for the night, the grass green and lush,
Our horses need feeding on the cream of that land,
Another fire we would kindle, the pans on the hook,
Mother would cook the best meal of that day,
And then we would talk of the things done that day,
We would bring Dad his fiddle, and he'd start to play,
Scottish hornpipes and Irish jigs, for he could play nice,
That music was sweet in the still of the night,
Then we would rest, counting the stars in the sky,
And dream of tomorrow in beautiful sleep.

Contents

List of Illustrations

Preface by the Editor

With the exception of the Prologue, and a few pages elsewhere in the book, this story was spoken by Gordon Boswell into a tape recorder and subsequently transcribed. The Prologue, part of Chapter One, and a very few pages elsewhere were written by him. The reader, then, is respectfully asked to consider the book as the spoken word, unscripted and unprepared, and not to judge it by the standards applied to written work.

Prologue

My name is Silvester Gordon Boswell, and my age is seventy-four. I am the son of Trafalgar Boswell, who died at Spalding in Lincolnshire at the age of ninety-four years and now lies at rest in Skegness churchyard beside my mother, Athaliah, who died in August 1920.

I am the grandson of Silvester Boswell, better known as Wester, spoken of numerous times by writers on Romanies and their language, and I have in my possession, given to me by my father, a medallion that was presented to Wester Boswell on New Year's Day 1875. On the one side it reads *Wester Boswell, a Grammarian of the Ancient Gypsy Language*; and on the other the same wording, only in Romany, which is: *Westarus Boshanok, Jinomeskro, Trustal o Poorokono Romanes*. The medal, my father told me, was presented to Wester at Barton-on-Humber, where he received most of his education in later years. He lies in Everton Cemetery, Liverpool.

My great-grandfather was Tyso Noname Boswell. When he was a baby his mother took him to be christened at church, and the minister asked her what name she had decided on for the child. She replied: 'Tyso Jehovah Boswell,' but when told that Jehovah could not be used and the reason why, she then said: 'He shall have no other name but Tyso Noname Boswell.'

Tyso Noname was a man well known all his life throughout the Romany tribes until the day he died at Tetford, on August the fifth, 1831. This was the time of the great Horncastle Horse Fair and Tetford was a good camping place. Tyso and his cousin, Edward Heron, had been to see to their horses and had collected some straw for their tents, when they were slain by lightning while sheltering from the storm in an old hovel; my father told me that even the laces of their boots were split.

Soon after the First War I had been at Horncastle Fair, and I decided to travel to Tetford with the horses I had left, taking the same road that my grandfather and his cousin had travelled many years before, with the intention of finding, if possible, the graves of these two men. After I had found a place to camp, and had made my horses safe, I took one horse to the blacksmith's shop directly opposite the church with the idea of contacting the minister.

It turned out that this was unnecessary, for in the forge the blacksmith, who was getting on in years, told me that the old man who was resting on a bench in the shop was his father, and it wasn't long before I had told him of my errand and asked him if in his lifetime he had heard about the death of these two people. Could he tell me where the grave was to be found?

'Aye,' he said, 'it happened in my father's time, for they used to bring their horses in this very shop to be shod.'

And he thought it a great occasion to be asked questions about these men's deaths, after so many years, and even more so that it was by the great-grandson of Tyso Noname Boswell.

He said: 'Now, my boy – go to the back of the church and you will see a big holly bush, and under it you will find twin gravestones.'

And sure enough, I did find them. The next day I cleaned and scraped the moss from the stones and found the dates and names.

That night I lay in my wagon, which I had moved to a rough bushy piece of common land with a bank beside it – just the place, I thought, where they would be likely to camp in those days. And in my mind I pictured the sorrow of my people at that time through the loss of these two good men, whose lives had been cut short with such tragic suddenness, one at fifty-two years and the other at fifty-six. The next day I had a feeling of satisfaction that I had paid my respects to their resting-place.

Prologue

In the early days of my great-great-grandfather and his tribes the mode of transport was pack donkeys and horses.

They lived in tents, which consisted of young ash or hazel saplings covered with felts or blankets or suchlike, and when they were on their travels, these *rods*, as we called the saplings, would be tied in two bundles on each side of the horse or donkey, and the bedding and any other things packed on top of the animals. Their way of getting a living then and for generations after was as tinsmiths, copper beaters, basket makers, and also by using the grinding forge. This had one wheel only – the frame being fitted with handles like wheelbarrow shafts and with two adjustable legs attached. This could be wheeled or carried on the back, and the business of grinding was carried out by a grindstone driven by a belt from a wheel turned by a treadle action. It was called a 'man-rider' owing to its being carried over stiles and gates.

When my great-grandfather Tyso became a man and had a wife and family he travelled with others around Portsmouth. Those were the days of the press gang, and it happened that with other unwary civilians he was taken for military service, with his cousin Edward Heron. Whether they were in camps or barracks during training I do not know; but their wives and families were allowed to be somewhere near their menfolk, with their tents and horses, and then, as now, the government was responsible for the dependants of soldiers, and this was where my grandfather, Silvester Boswell, received his first lessons: the first instance of any education among Romanies. This schooling interested him enough to further his knowledge, and as time went on enabled him to be spoken of as 'a grammarian of the ancient Gypsies and their language'.[1]

There was one case of horse stealing when two of Tyso's relatives were convicted and transported: one to Australia and the other to America.

In the first case, the man who was convicted was quite young and had not long been wed. After serving his time for a great many years abroad he returned to England as an old

[1] See Editor's Notes, p. 193.

man, and tramped the country for over three years in search of his wife. He eventually found her on South Shore, Blackpool: a stopping place well known to Romanies for many years. When the couple talked things over they agreed to live together and did so for the rest of their lives: the wife having remained faithful during all those years her husband had been abroad.

As for the man who was sent to America, a very interesting fact was discovered by one of my elder brothers who went to Canada in 1902 and eventually crossed to America. He came across a family of Gypsies in America by the name of Boswell and was soon on good terms with them and about the year 1916 he married one of the daughters of the family, whose name was Phoebe, and when he came over to England between World Wars One and Two, during conversation with my father, it became clear that my brother's wife's great-grandfather and Tyso Boswell were cousins.

Now going back to the origins of my people, according to the teachings of my father and grandfather and great-grandfather and it's been handed down to me: we believe that when Jesus was crucified and the two thieves with him, we believe it was a Gypsy they went to to make these nails, and that they was made of copper. But the Gypsy people found what these nails were for, and instead of giving them four nails they only give them three – one of them managed to escape with one of these nails. And the Gentiles have been looking for that nail ever since. And it has been this search that has led to the persecution of the Gypsy. And I believe that it's just coming to the point when they're finding that nail, and they are realizing that the Gypsies done a *good* turn by taking it away instead of adding it to the other three.

That's my belief. That's what I've been taught.[2]

1

Childhood

I WAS born on the twenty-fifth of February 1895, at South Shore, Blackpool, and until my father's death in 1949 he was always telling me, when he spoke about the weather, that the worst year he remembered for snow was the year I was born. He often said the snow had drifted higher than the telegraph wires, and horses and carts could travel over the frozen snow. Many horses and cattle were trapped and frozen to death in that year.

I was born in a rod tent with a 'barricade' to it. It was made of ash rods or saplings, with a ridge pole that joined the rods together, and that was the rear half. Joined to the front of this was the barricade, which was much bigger all round. The whole tent was covered with wool blankets. My father got these blankets usually from paper mills: mostly in Blackburn, Lancs. It was the material that was on the rollers for the paper pulp to be rolled on. Some of these blankets were twenty or thirty feet long and ten feet wide, and the colour varied according to the paper that had gone on them. They made the best tents, too.

Father was a good man at making a tent. And the type of tent I was born in, and used for years after the time I am talking about, was thirty feet long, twelve feet wide and ten feet high. The skewers we used for the tent was either log wood, like mahogany, or dog wood, but especially the long thorns pulled off the blackthorn or sloe bush. When the bark was scraped off these and they were dried Father would fry them in mutton fat – and they lasted for years, too.

At the back half of this tent would be, first, a foot of clean straw and a good piece of carpet over this. In the front barricade would be a big stone slab for the fire kettles to stand on, and along the sides would be some seats to sit on: usually orange boxes, covered with good rugs or blankets. The compartments of these orange boxes made fine storage for boots, clothes and other things.

Our tablecloth was spread on the carpet at the back, and all the family would sit around it with our legs doubled up and, in silence, Mother would give us our meals. I don't remember ever sitting down to a meal without Mother saying Grace for us all. I remember it to this day. Always she said: 'We thank Thee Lord for what we are about to receive, and bless it to our bodies, and sanctify our souls for Thy service, Amen.'

It may seem odd for a Gypsy to do this, but it's the truth.[3]

My mother was one of the best-natured women I ever knew: not only to her family but many others living today say the same of her.

Even at the time of my birth, besides the tent we had a good Gypsy wagon, with the wheels run outside.[4] It was the second Gypsy wagon made by Tom Tongs, of Manchester. It had a good stove and oven in it, with an all-brass front, made by Beard and Sons of Colchester, and it was considered a palace on wheels at that time. It was the next improvement after the two-wheeled cart, or tilted cart, that was used by Romanies that could afford them. In fact there were only two Gypsy wagons at Blackpool at the time. The other belonged to Bill Townsend. He was rather a wealthy Gypsy man, and his wife was called Hutty Townsend and she was an Italian Gypsy, and she used to keep parakeets; and people could put pennies in the slot and the birds would pull tickets out of slots, you know, and there was little pieces on them – your fortune.

I was about four years old when my father made a fire of coke to burn in a tent. He was the first Gypsy man ever to do so. I've heard him say many times that many people on the South Shore thought he was crazy – some said he was a genius to find such a useful secret, for remember the usual fire for a tent before that was sticks or logs from the tree or hedge bottom. He told me coke was so plentiful at that time that it was fourpence per hundredweight, and that winter he bought a ton of coke. Others on the South Shore thought he was a millionaire – until they knew the price, and then all had it from then onwards.

That tent had all the comfort and warmth that anyone could wish for in those days of my childhood. A swinging oil-lamp hanging from the ridge-pole had a shade over it too. Our beds and blankets all folded at the back of the tent, and most were coloured Scotch blankets. They lasted many years I can remember. And always a great Paisley shawl covered the lot.

A big willow basket with a lid on was at one side for cups, plates and dishes, but foodstuff was kept in the wagon kettle-box or pan-box. This was under the back of the wagon: a big box with shelves and doors to it. It was the pantry, as you might say. Mother's crockery was always of the very best. She never used anything white: never a white cup or saucer or white plates.[5] As far back as I can remember she always had lovely crockery ware, such as the Cries of London pattern which we called 'Grinders' pots, and, yes, Crown Derby. Mother's home was always renowned for her Crown Derby, and of course many other Gypsies had it too.

In those days, when this tent was at South Shore, Mother used it in the summer season for her palmistry work – with a big board over the door with her name on it. She always had good seasons, as our position was a good one – near the old switchback, in the run of the people. But when the summer season was over we would move to a different place for the winter after travelling, perhaps to Preston. I went to school there for a time. We stopped at Fishergate, on a sort of tip. It was a regular stopping place for many families for many years. Or it might have been Manchester, or Liverpool – Aintree too. My Uncle Kenza stopped there for many years with his family, too.

But South Shore, Blackpool, was the beginning of my memories.

As a little boy of less than four years, with my younger brother Lewis (we were never apart), life for us and for several other Gypsy children related to us was fun and play from morning till night. You see, we could play in the sand all day round our home, and bathe in the sea when we liked all the summer through when thousands of other children would only get the privilege one day a year. We had all the sunshine from morning to night and we could play with hardly any clothes on: we were as brown as berries and as fit as fiddles. This in itself was something that other children didn't get. We were free, and only came home when we wanted something to eat. And it was always there for us – Mother was waiting – never an angry word from her as I remember – and then off again, probably to play with the fairies over the sandhills.

I dare say now you are going to call me light in the head.

I have played with the fairies on South Shore, Blackpool, and so did many other Gypsy children at that time. Many are living today that will back me up in this. Sometimes my sisters, Laura and Linda, brother Lewis and myself, would land home a bit late, and Mother would ask us where we had been so long, and the answer would be: 'We have been playing with the fairies!' She never called us silly, or said: 'There is no such thing as a fairy.' Because we paid them a visit most days. If we were getting a bit of a bore to her she would say: 'Get off and go and play with the fairies!' and we would go. It was always the same place too: several hundred yards over the dunes at the back of the tents and wagons to some sandhills covered with star grass we called it: a long reed grass. This was a regular routine with us children, and this was going on not just for a day or a week but all the time we stayed as children, and when we travelled after the summer season and returned to the South Shore we would be off to the fairies, and they in turn would be there too.

I must say again: people must now be sure I am a head case, and need medical attention, but I am not ashamed to say that I and my brother Lewis, and sisters Laura, Linda and Ida, have played with the fairies on Blackpool South Shore.

Our lives at that time was continuous happiness and play, and when it was time for bed we slept and had beautiful dreams which we would tell each other next day, of lovely pony foals, and donkeys perhaps ... Not the type of dreams many *Gaujo*[6] children had – I mean when their parents told them if they didn't go to sleep the black man or the Gypsy would come and get them.

There were many other Romany families beside us too. There was Ada Lee – wife of Tobias Boswell, and their family Daisy, Clara, Kitten and Ada. There was old Tom – he had a little tent all on his own. He was a very old man. I used to have a peep at him sometimes: sitting cross-legged in front of a little fire-bucket, sometimes roasting a few snails (*bouries*) or a hedgehog (*hotchie*), for he liked them. He was too old to get these himself, but many boys used to find them for him. He had sat down so long that whenever he stood up he was so bow-legged a pig could have run through his legs.

There was old Gypsy Sarah, and old Noah Young and his wife Goosey, then two daughters Lotty and Beatrice; there was old Isaac and Sinfie Heron, old Bill Townsend and his wife Hutty, Adolphus Smith and his wife Sibey and their family, Arthur, Frank, Adie and Tilly. Adolphus was my mother's uncle. There was my Uncle Wallace and his wife Jemima and family: Lesley, Gladys, Muriel and Mona.

These families came to the South Shore just for the summer months – apart from a few families who remained there permanently.

My Uncle Kenza and his wife Menia used to have a palmistry tent on the South Shore, and they had a coke fire and an eight-gallon boiler on the fire, cooking dinners and so on. The girls would do it. And they was cooking some rabbits and some dumplings in this big boiler and, well, a gang of boys and girls come up, and the girls wanted their fortunes told and they went to Aunt Menia's tent. And while the boys were waiting for the girls – it was the time, you know, when everybody wore a straw hat and a cane – well they was interested in what was in this boiler and they lifted up the lid. And they found out that there was some suet dumplings and some rabbits' legs sticking out of the water and they stirred it up with their walking-sticks – and they eventually put two or three handfuls of sand in among these rabbits and these suet dumplings.

And the daughters – Ettie and Gertie – saw them and shouted to their father to get up to what these boys were doing and Uncle Henry got up from his sleep and ran to this boiler and he see a leg of rabbit sticking out of the water and he got hold of it and he ran after these boys and he flung the rabbit at one and he hit the boy in the back of the head with it! But part of the rabbit stuck to his hand and he had a badly scalded hand for weeks.

But they was like that years ago. When the girls would be in the rod tents, having their fortunes told, the boys used to put their ears to the tent blankets to hear what was said. But you could see their shadow on the blankets – from inside the tent, and it was the day of the hat-pins, and if one of us little children or a boy was there we would get this hat-pin and stick it in their ear-hole. That would shift them from the tent!

There was my Uncle Wallace too – he was older than my father – he's been dead many years now, but he was a bit of a character and he used to go to a fair and get a glass or two of beer and get the worse for drink. And he went to Ormskirk Fair, in Lancashire, which was a permanent horse fair at that time, and he got himself into trouble and they pulled him inside.

And he didn't get tried the next day – there was no magistrate or something of the kind. But they never stripped him of his money, or his knife he always carried, you know, or his pipe and tobacco – they let him have that; and early next morning – I expect he'd been asleep and woke up – he was cold in this cell. Well at that time the prisoners used to be fed with a wooden spoon and a wooden basin, and he got his knife out and split up this wooden basin and the wooden spoon into shavings and he made himself a fire on the stone floor. And the smoke came through the bars of the door and the fire alarm went off and the whole police station was upset about this fire alarm. Somebody went along and unlocked the door, and found the cell was full of smoke, and he got himself seven days extra in the cell for disfiguring the police goods.

But when Father got ready for travelling in the spring we were all delighted. The fourteenth of February was his day – the time to start washing our wagon and hawking-lorry[7] and cleaning the harness. Horses would be shod at the blacksmith ready to move as soon as the weather was right. Father was a very particular man about cleanliness with all his goods, and all the family helped with this because we knew it meant going on the road: fresh stopping places, lovely green lanes and wide corners, plenty of grass for the horses and plenty of sport for myself and brother Lewis.

There would be fishing in ponds for eels, newts or lizards, tiddlers or gudgeon in a stream; bows and arrows or certainly a catapult. We were crack shots with these. And while we were tending our horses down a beautiful lane – in those days of unspoiled England, full of violets, primroses and wild roses – we would make a stick fire and roast a potato or two, and sometimes a bird on a spit. These are the times that stand out in my memory even now. And I'm certain no Gypsy children since the 1914 War finished has had the times that we, our family, had in my young days.

While this was happening with us my mother would be out hawking with the horse and lorry with all sorts of things to sell: wicker armchairs, carpets and rugs, coconut door mats and many other household things; and perhaps Father would be with her, or a brother, to attend to the horse. This was my job after I grew up a bit. I have been with her hawking when I was about eight years old – to hold the horse when she went to the houses and shops. I was happy doing this job for her, and when I wanted some dinner she always got it for me. If she called at a big gentleman's house, in those days there was always a lady cook employed, and Mother would ask for something for her little boy who was looking after the horse outside and she never missed getting me pie, or something very nice to eat.

More often than not, when the old English gentry were living the lives of which they have been deprived since times have changed, Mother would have given to her many things that would surprise people today, such as chicken, hams, venison and game of all sorts – besides having done business at the same house or hall.

Probably Dad would get some work there in putting cane bottoms in chairs and sofas. Lots of work like this Mother got for Dad and brother Nathan to do. Both were crack tradesmen at it, and Father could make a nice basket too. He would cut his willows from a willow bed, peel and dye them, and make bread baskets for the table. Most homes had them in those days: a round basket with loops of willow round it. He would make a nice fishing basket too, for he liked fishing. He was never without a good rod and tackle.

And when the day's hawking was done we would land home, and everything was ready and clean for tea, for sisters Linda and Laura would have to have things ready for us. During the day they would do some washing, for they both had their own washtubs made out of the half beer-barrel, all polished; or they would be cleaning and shining the brass on the stove in the wagon, or the little candlesticks, and always the copper kettles and water cans were bright.

Both Linda and Laura were good needleworkers, and both made lovely lace. They would have a rag doll each, and they would make clothes for them.

And a bit more play for Lewis and me. It might be marbles, or a top. With peg tops we were good. Or we might play with our cart made of a Hudson's soap box on mail-cart wheels, painted. Dad would let us have a cart: it was about the only thing we were allowed to carry – that and a rod for fishing. These were the only toys we had, and even when we were young I don't remember having toys to play with.

There were no bought toys for us. Lewis and I could play with a cardboard shoe-box for hours on end, or amuse ourselves with a branch pulled from a hedge and put it between our legs as if riding a horse and run up the road cutting up the dust. Or sometimes we would have 'school' with Linda as 'teacher', doing sums and reading, and Laura would play on the small organ we had in the wagon. She could play well – and the Irish harp too.

And then we would move on again and the next place for us was ... school. School, if only for a week or two, and most of our happiness seemed to come to an end. We were not put on the register book. If the schoolmaster said: 'What standard were you in last school?', and we answered: 'Standard Three!', it was: 'Put him in Standard Two, teacher – they're not here for long.'

This is what always seemed to happen, and it was always big boy in a class of little ones, and my sisters too. We were called *dunces*, and we all had a fight first day and every day alike. Next school we would say: 'Standard Four', one class higher than we had been ever, and it would be Standard Three then, and we told lies to do it and we were told never to tell no lies. I'm sure it was at school when we started telling our first serious lies – in trying to get into the class that we were entitled to be in.

But we knew it would end when we moved on, and were happy and free again.

Of course my father was just a shade above the average Gypsy man. He had his horses, and he was a live wire, and my mother used to get money and so we had plenty of comfort. Mother and Father used to sleep in the wagon with the little children, and the boys used to sleep in this big barricade tent.

Mother had a big signboard, and I remember it was the time when the South African War finished, and the soldiers came home and there was one or two stray ones used to come and sleep in the front 'amusements' – probably been on the beer or something like that.

My father, at that time, had what they called a *camera obscura*. It was a six-squared building, and there was a white sheet inside, and a mirror at the top, and if anybody lost a child on the beach they could come to our *camera obscura*

and Father used to charge 'em sixpence, and you could regu-
late this mirror on the top and say: 'Is this your child?' and
she could pick that child out. And my father would keep a
Gypsy boy – a little Gypsy boy – to show her where that
particular part was, and they were so pleased that my father
used to get money like this.

He had another contraption. He had one of the first
gramophones, and he used to set it outside of our tent, or on
a box on the front board of the wagon, in his spare time, and
he had a big long bar with a horn on it and swung up on a
chain, and he used to put these round records on, and it used
to say: 'Edison Bell Records'. One of the songs was 'Come
Back to Dixie' and there was all types of old Coon songs, and
we had quite a lot of these records, and Father used to go
round with his hat, or a little bag, and collect money. That
was the first gramophone I'd ever seen, and a lot of other
people had seen either, and I've heard my father say it cost
seven pounds.

When the season was in full swing he was manager of the
Figure Eight, the Scenic Railway, and my brother Nathan
was keeping the cars in repair, and me and my brother
Lewis, we used to go under this big switchback, when we
could see him, and shout: '*Daddus*' – or 'Daddy! Give us a
penny, Daddy!' and he used to throw us a penny down and
we'd go away and spend it. And when we wanted another
penny we used to go to another pair of Gypsy girls that were
relations of ours: Etty and Gertie, and they was afraid of
mice, and if we went for a penny and they wouldn't give us
one we used to go and find a mouse in the sandhills and as
soon as ever they saw this mouse they'd shout: 'Take it away!
Take it away!' and we used to get our penny.

Now another amusement on the beach at that time as I
remember – and I was only about four years old – was one
old set of Gallopers (a roundabout), and they belonged to old
Charlie Oathwaite. And there used to be a figure-board, and
if you rode on the outside – on the third row of horses – and
you reached out, there was some rings on this figure-board,
and if you could put your finger in a ring, and show it to the

man who took the money, you could get an extra ride. And there was another sort of Galloper track – but with bicycles on it, three abreast – and the people used to get on this and pedal themselves along, and the more people that was on – the faster they went. And that was a penny a ride.

That was about the only amusements there was on South Shore, Blackpool, at that particular time – apart, of course, from Gypsy women with the palmistry business. And I don't remember anything else apart from the old bathing machines that used to be pulled with a horse, backwards and forwards.

But this roundabout, or particular set of Gallopers that was there: we used to go and have rides on it when we wanted to, and one day we was waiting for it to slow down and it hit Lewis's leg – the surrounding board did – and broke his leg in two places. And he was taken to the doctor.

They put his leg in splints, and we carried him home. They didn't keep in him hospital, because Father wouldn't allow us to be in hospital. We'd already been taken away with measles, and we'd had to be taken away to Kirkham. Father wouldn't let us go unless he went with us, and he stayed with us in the hospital until we was better. It was at this time that Father made us the truck with the wheels of a mail-cart, and we used to put Lewis on it, and I'd go pushing him and pulling him about the sand and people used to say: 'Oh what have you done to your leg, little boy?' and we'd get more pennies than ever then, because people used to sympathize with a little boy with his leg in a splint. So it was a paying concern, that broken leg.

And when the season was over and Father would travel, probably we'd travel to Preston and have a week or a fortnight or a month there, and if the weather was open we'd probably go further down the country to Freckleton, perhaps to Liverpool, or even Manchester. We'd keep on the road while the weather was right, and then we would settle down and have a wonderful Christmas.

Mother would cook her turkey, and Father Christmas

would come to us. It was a great time, was Christmas, for us. We used to love to go and get our own ivy off trees, and decorate our tent. My sisters made chains with coloured paper. We had very happy times at Christmas.

In our wagon we had a stove that was well known in wagon time. But Mother used to cook outside in a Dutch oven: an eight-gallon cast iron boiler – and we could put a turkey in that, and put it over a stick fire, or next to a stick fire, and it would roast and roast and roast until it was absolutely brown and beautiful. We used to baste it with the fat that was made and with what was put into it: a big slice of bacon on top so that it was continually dripping with fat.

That's how we used to do our cooking.

I think most old-fashioned Gypsy people like us wouldn't be without a Dutch oven. There were three different sizes. You could either fry in them, or roast in them: because there was an iron lid on them and a sort of ventilator on top, and when it got very hot the steam used to come through a little whistle. You could set it on the brands of the fire, and cover it over with the brands, and you'd have roast beef, or you could bake a frying-pan cake in it: all Gypsy people never was without a frying-pan cake – either a currant cake or a shortcake, probably an inch thick. I've seen Mother stand them up like pennies before the fire, and it was beautiful when you open them up and put butter between – it was good.

I don't remember being short of food.

I think we was a very plentiful family. I think it was because my father was a live wire. I believe he was a business-man with a horse. He could get work, if we were out hawking. The moment we left Blackpool we'd be loaded with blankets and rugs and coconut mats and enamel ware, and at the end of the day Mother would exchange some enamel pans for meat from the butcher. Or you'd go to a grocery shop: 'Buy something off me, missus – I'll spend the money with you!'

We used to live tip-top.

I've known my mother to bring a big bullock's head home,

and put it in the boiler and make potted meat out of it. And that used to stay in the kettle-box of the wagon. We always had full and plenty, and then we wasn't above finding a pheasant.

Boyhood

Queen Victoria died in 1901, and I always think that that particular year was the turning-point in the life of my father and mother and our family.

Because Mother and Father was converted at Liverpool by John Wesley Baker, a Gypsy evangelist, and Gypsy Rodney Smith. And my father – he used to drink: he'd go to a public house and play his fiddle, and amuse people, and of course he'd come home tipsy at times and so on, which didn't suit Mother – he signed the pledge. And I have his old pledge card now, signed on the nineteenth of August 1901.

Well that particular winter, when we was at Preston, it was decided that my father and mother would never return to Blackpool again with their family. They considered it a wicked life – with the amusements, and the Sunday work, and so on.

It was a turning-point in the life of my people and they took life very seriously, and intended to take our family right out of the amusements of Blackpool. There was eight boys and three girls of us.

And my father took to the road in earnest. He travelled all over the British Isles, and of course he travelled in Scotland and Ireland.

I had two brothers born in Ireland: twin brothers. One died in Ireland, one died in Scotland. My brother Eden was christened at Inverness, and his godfather was Bishop Eden. But my father, in 1901, took seriously to his Gypsy life again, and we travelled all over the West of England.

We would have the big wagon – the big four-wheeler – and we boys used to build up the eight-rod tent every night wherever we travelled. The boys would sleep in the tent. And later when the boys got men and done business for themselves and yet remained single, they bought a wagon, a light wagon, sort of like a bow-topped wagon – there wasn't many about then, not in that part of the country, it was all square wagons.

As for the tent – normally the eight-rod tent was a round tent, and we used to put these rods together and strap them up and put them under the bed of our wagon with two stirrup straps, and the blankets used to be rolled up and put on the rack of the wagon. And when we stopped at night the boys had to build their tent up and get a bundle of straw to put in the tent, and we were able to make a stick fire – or a coke fire – outside, and we would have tea and settle down and get ourselves to bed. And up next morning we'd pull our tent down if Father was in that mood to travel on, if the place didn't suit him. But if we got on a common anywhere, we used to stop.

Probably at that time we would keep two very good horses for pulling our big wagon, which would be good and quiet. My father kept these special animals to pull his wagon. When you've got a big ship of a wagon as we call them – weighing probably two ton or fifty hundredweight, and they were big high wagons – the horse that went in those shafts had to be perfectly quiet, with Mother sitting inside, and probably two or three little children. Above the horse's head there would be the bow of the big wagon; if they could see through their blinkers some horses wouldn't face the road: they'd throw themselves down, or kick a wagon to pieces. Well, you had to have a perfect horse for that job, and once you found a good animal that us children was attached to and was quiet – well that horse was kept.

But it would normally be a mare, because when we was keeping it we would breed from it at the same time, and we would breed a foal, and when we were going to have a foal we would be just as excited as some children would be expecting a baby brother or sister. And when that foal come we loved it, and the day it was born we never ceased to look after it. It was at our wagon door; it was fed out of a saucer, it fed on our bread.[8] It used to lay down, and we would cover it up, thinking it wanted to go to bed!

And our foals were never broken in. I've known us to have a foal a fortnight old, and while Father and Mother was away we would put the harness on it, and we would make it as though we was travelling, because as children we used to play tents and wagons at that time. We used to work these foals, and probably get the traces on them and hook them on to a tin tray or something and we used to let the foal pull us about. And Father was very much surprised when he come home and he used to roust us: 'You'll ruin that foal – you'll hurt it!'

But we wouldn't hurt it. We was very kind to it you know. We was just kidding ourselves that we was travelling, and if we couldn't get the foal in the shafts, which many times we couldn't, we'd pull the cart ourselves. We would have our own little set of rods and we'd probably travel in this corner of the field or further down the lane or common and under a bush we would build a little tent up and we'd even play husbands and wives and kids falling out like we'd heard other people. And we would make a stick fire and we would boil a kettle, and we'd go and fetch something to eat, and the little girls used to put a little basket on their arm and go along the hedges probably blackberrying or picking leaves and say they was going out hawking and they was bringing the food home.

We had marvellous times. Never any children today or the past forty years even up to this side of the '14 War – no children was born that since then ever had the times we had as children. We lived so close to nature. We didn't want any plastic toys. We had our mail-cart or our little trotting-cart. We travelled about. We tended the horses up the road. We made fires. We took two or three potatoes and roasted them. We had our catapult too! We could kill a bird, and plenty of rabbits about. And we knew every bird there was. Tits, wrens, goldfinches, bullfinches, linnets – we knew every bird there was, and we could tell by their eggs what they was.

And then of course we used to go fishing. We always had a fishing rod or a long cane under the bed of the wagon wherever we used to go. We used to go fishing for eels *and* we would get some: we could go and fish in any pond and get lots of nice fish. And when we couldn't get proper fish, there was gudgeons about and a whole lot of little tiddlers.

Our life was beautiful. That is honest talk to you. It's hard for people to believe but it was wonderful. When I see little children today with the stuff that they're buying them today to amuse themselves with – they use it *one* day – *we* were satisfied when those things wasn't there. Didn't exist. Why, a cardboard box would have to be made into a cart for a younger brother, or a child, with a piece of string tied to it. He was happy with that. At Christmas-time, even when I had my children, I used to make a toy – a wheelbarrow or a little cart. I had a bit of wood and I used to saw short pieces off, save every one of them, and they was blocks and my children used to build with them. I never went to the shop for a toy.

We had a bitch, a good one that could kill a hare or a rabbit and fetch it home for us, and one that could find a hedgehog; and it would have puppies and we loved the puppies. We never gave them away. We didn't sell them. If we did sell, if we did part with them, they went to our relations because the character of that particular dog was like the character of a racehorse today. It was doing a hard job. It was necessary in life. It would kill a hare or a rabbit.

But the horses we would have to pull our wagons: I remember we had a Welsh mare called Star – a blue-roan mare. We had her for years, and a big grey mare that come from a mill. She used to go on the side because of course our wagon weighed about fifty hundredweight. It took a good horse to pull it up and down the country, and many a time we used to keep a spare horse with a collar and hames on to put a third horse on up the hill.

My oldest brother Nathan was probably fifteen years older than me, and he was a man when I was a boy and there was other ones besides. I'm the youngest boy now living. They would all have a cob or two and probably we would have eight or ten horses and ponies and so we had a road-full of tackle.

And everything had to be cleaned. Harness: it had to be cleaned. If we pulled on a muddy place, my father brought out his bucket and his brush; and if there was any dirt on the fellies[9] when we pulled them on the road, one of us boys had to get that water and wash those fellies round. Father would be very particular. When we've been on a common and it's been nice weather, we've pulled the wheels on four little pieces of board and my sister has black-leaded the tyres of our wagon – that was her job.

My two sisters – Linda and Laura – cleaned up the wagon and prepared everything for when we used to come home from hawking at three o'clock in the day, and Mother would bring the meat and the bread and all like that and we'd have a marvellous tea. Or perhaps I wouldn't go out with Mother; perhaps Lewis would; perhaps one of the other boys would go out or Father would go out.

Mother had probably seen a horse the day before, and she would come home and say; 'Algar – I've seen an old horse – a man wants to sell it.' Of course Mother could find a horse. She could *buy* one, but she wasn't allowed by my Father. Mother used to make the running, but Father would finish the business off. She always kept my father in a man's place. And that's as far as she would go. But she got into conversation with people when horses were for sale and when there was money Father used to go and buy. He couldn't help it. He was like me.

And when I was a child it was quite easy to get a living. There wasn't the responsibility that there is today with Travelling people or Gypsy people.

A man would have a horse, and he'd have a foal with it, or another old horse: he would mind it up a lane, and his wife would go into the village or the town with her hawking, and she'd sell a bit of lace and get a contact with the woman and tell her fortune for two shillings or a shilling or half-a-crown: she would take a few shillings and come walking home by three o'clock. Because if a woman wasn't home by three o'clock in those days there was something evidently wrong. It was a rule with the old Gypsy people for the

women to show their faces to their husbands and their home
at three o'clock in the day, and the husband would be home
with a fire or something ready.[10]

People kept a dog that could kill a hare or rabbit, and a
man could keep a catapult and shoot a bird; he could snare a
partridge, he could shoot a pheasant with a catapult. And
there was plenty of grass for a horse to eat – they'd go from
one end of the year to the other and never cost a shilling.
Things was plentiful. These were the people that knew all
the nicks and corners in the way of life – and they wasn't
doing anybody any harm. It was a free life. But people can't
imagine today that there was such a life as what there was in
those days. And there was time for a laugh – time for
pleasure in our humble way.

I remember we travelled down to Cheshire, and then we
went into Shropshire, and we stopped outside of Shrewsbury
on a common called Berrington Green and there was a lot of
Gypsy families there. There were some Locks and some
Loveridges and Lovells, and some Welsh Gypsies, some
better off than others; some was very poor, mixed up with
other classes of people.[11] But it was a regular stopping
place.

And John Wesley Baker had his mission tent there, and
my father built it up for him. He had a secretary called Mr
Zebedee. He was a bachelor, was John Wesley Baker, and he
stayed on Berrington Green and I believe he died there.

He wasn't a Gypsy, and according to what I think he
wasn't liked by the Gypsy people, and his business went
away from him. Of course Esmeralda Lock (who lived for
years with Romany-Rye Groome, was it?) – when Groome
died, she went back to John Wesley Baker and she died with
him, or near him, at Berrington Green. She was a very
beautiful woman, a very beautiful Gypsy woman. My father
remembered her but I don't. I can't remember seeing
her.[12]

And I remember my father buying a lot of lovely horse
rugs, and a pony, and another big horse; and my father gave
the pony to me and Lewis – a sort of kids' pony. Pony with a

lot of hair on it. And as we travelled along the road we used to take turns riding. It was a beautiful little pony – one of the first I ever had, apart from a donkey that Father gave two-and-six for and give to us.

On Berrington Common our play was fishing in ponds for eels and lizards, or anything that would go on a ha'penny hook and line (that was the price in those days) tied to a mop cane which my mother would sell off the lorry while out hawking, with a jute head on for cleaning windows. We would catch linnets, bullfinches and other birds to give to my older brothers to sell for us, and make little tents and fires, and have our Hudson's soap box on wheels for a cart. We would pull our tent down and travel over the common, and build it up again, at the same time keeping Father's horses from straying on to the road or rambling too far away. But our real work was to clean two sets of harness every Saturday, and wash our hawking-lorry down, and our wages were a penny-ha'penny a week for this.

Of course we were crack hands at marbles and peg tops and whip tops. We liked the ha'penny 'flying Dutchman'. I've put several through a window, and a few my mother had to pay for. I went to a little school in Berrington, but I don't think I learned much there.

We also travelled in Worcestershire, stopping for some time at Hartlebury Common. Here many families of Romanies stopped for the fruiting season, which provided plenty of work for them. There were many children to play with, but it was still tending horses in case they strayed too far or on to the road. Always the play was building little rod tents, and moving over the common where our horses were grazing the best of the grass. We tied our horses up at night, for safety.

The next stopping place I remember was Welshpool. It was considered a good market town for horses and ponies, and hawking and all that. But we were moving all over. Aberystwyth – where we saw more ponies on the mountains than we ever saw in our lives – Abergavenny and Hereford. And then we left the West Country: we moved right over to the

London area: to such places as Wanstead Flats, Woolwich Common, Blackheath and Romford.

And there was everything free.

Old England was a wonderful place then, but now it seems to me like a police state. Wherever you go nowadays you're doing wrong, or you're attempting to do wrong, or you're about to do wrong and what then? When we've done all these wrong things we are just going where we should go, where we have a right to be. People has commandeered our common lands to build on. They've taken our by-ways, our lovely lanes away from us. And where *are* these people that's left on the roads today? They've got nowhere to go. You can't travel the roads. The traffic is too strong. So we've got to revert back to tin cans and iron trailers and that is everything on wheels. When we have an animal – and I still have them and I still like them – we have to put it in a trailer to take it home to avoid accidents. It's all restrictions. Old England isn't like it was when I was a child.

Travelling

ONE time we stopped near the old varnish works at Barkingside. At that time several families stayed there permanently. It was a dangerous place to leave our horses at night, and I remember well that my father and my brothers tied the halters of the horses to their ankles, and lay beside the fire in the door of the rod tent, for at that time many good horses were missing. For, horses being the main form of transport, it was not difficult to dock a horse, then take his mane off, clip his heels out – and then he would be looked upon in London as one of the thousands of other horses that had been sold from the London horse or bus companies as surplus animals, and if we had not taken care of our horses they may have been added to the list of other stolen ones. This was happening for years in London. A good horse was always fair game to a horse stealer at that time, and it would take a good man – even a dealing man – to recognize his own horses.

My father – yes, and even my grandfather and my Uncle Wallace – they could all fight as boys. They used to fight on boxing booths, perhaps for a few shillings, and they was very active men. My father, he died at the age of ninety-eight and he never ailed at all; he would stand no nonsense from no man in his time. And I remember, when we was stopping there at Barkingside, near the varnish works that was a traditional old stopping place for Travelling people, on that site was an old London Gypsy man by the name of Liney Silks that was well known for his racy clothes and his big watch and chain. And he was an old fighting man.

When anybody fresh pulled on to the ground with his horses and caravans, Liney Silks used to get on top of a big muck-heap – probably stable manure at that time – and he would stand on this muck-heap and flap his wings like a cockerel and he would 'Cock-a-doodle-do!', and that meant he was cock of the ground, you see. And they was itching for someone to challenge him.

Well when we pulled on this ground, and he flapped his wings and he 'Cock-a-doodle-do!' a time or two, my father inquired what it was for. And Liney Silks said that any Travelling man that pulled on this ground could get up on the muck-heap and 'Cock-a-doodle-do!' and he would take him up on the subject.

But my father said: 'Now, you've told me you're Cock of the North, and you've been flapping your wings: get your clothes off!'

And Liney Silks didn't last long with my father, and my father he got on the hill and *he* 'Cock-a-doodle-do!' And it was spoken about down in the London country for many years.

From Barkingside we moved to Romford, or just on the outskirts. They called it by the name of Mauney's Estate: lots of woodlands and a good place for horses to graze. It was common land at that time, and there were a few Travellers that stayed there during our stay. One family was named Cumbers. Old Sonny they called the father, and there were two little girls in that family: Olive and Phyllis, and they made good playmates for my brother Lewis and my three sisters Laura, Linda and Ida, and Adelaide my cousin, who lost her mother when she was nine days old and my mother took her and for many years we all thought she was our own sister.[13]

We went to school there – at Mauney Road School they called it. It was a big school. None of us was happy there, but we had to go all the same. Looking back on those days, the lads in our school were a rough lot, sons of coster parents and the like. The old master was a bad-tempered case. He had a King Edward beard, and spent most of his time giving the lads the cane. Not only on their hands: he would bend you over a desk and lay it on thick and heavy. He hadn't much patience with us at all.

And of course the cock of the School had to have a battle

with the Gypsy boys, so we had to defend ourselves at all times. Not many days passed without a fight. If I won one, brother Lewis would lose his and that made me look for the one that beat him and so it went on. My sisters would have their share of battles too. We got the 'Gypsy, Gypsy, live in a tent, can't afford to pay your rent!' This was one of the worst schools we were sent to. I think it was because it was so big, and so many children. We seemed for ever in trouble – all because we were Gypsies and looked different from the others.

At that time hundreds of Russian ponies were shipped over, and most of them were corralled in the old Caledonian Market, in the pens where cattle were held. The best were bought by the dealers who supplied the collieries with pit ponies, and the rest went to the public. My father and brothers (I was too young) would go there and buy some every week: not many – three or six at times. Dad liked a big horse. He would go to the Elephant and Castle auction, and Barbican auction. These were the main places at that time to buy, and then we would graze them until we sold them at a horse fair or to a private buyer.

Romford still sticks out in my memory as the worst and most unhappy school any of us young ones of the family went to. I still remember taking our dinners in little canvas bags and hanging them up in the cloakroom, and at lunch-time our dinner was pinched and we had to go without. If we reported it – well, it meant another fight after school. Outside the gates there was always a roast-potato man with his cart, and we could buy a real big spud for a farthing, and salt and vinegar in it too; so we would keep a farthing in reserve in case we lost our lunch. This farthing was given us by our mother and father after we told them about the loss of our dinners.

And I'm sure that we had nicer things in our bags: thick currant pancakes Mother made in the pan (and butter in the middle too), and home-made cake. Most of the poorer boys' dinner was bread and jam, wrapped in newspaper in those days – with print twice as big as today and much blacker, and it used to come off on the bread and jam too, but they ate it alright.

Some of the boys told to get their hair cut came the next day with their heads like the furrows of a ploughed field: all gaps. If the master asked who'd cut their hair it was always their mothers. Lewis and I had our hair cut by my oldest brother, Nathan, with the horse clippers: all the lot off, no fringe left on at all. I often think we looked like a pair of convicts – all nose and no hair.

In my opinion – if that school hasn't altered since – I bet they never turned out a Member of Parliament from it.

Our next really long stay was at Eastwood, near Southend. There were then many real Romanies there on the Bohemia Estate, as it was called. There were Buckleys, Lees, plenty of Smiths – mostly related to Gypsy Rodney Smith, the evangelist. He stayed with our family for some time: he was conducting missions in Southend.

We young ones went to school at Eastwood with several other Gypsy children. We had a real happy time there – both at school and at play. We would go at night with a little policeman's bull's-eye lamp and catch sparrows, blackbirds and thrushes in the hedges, and if we got enough Mother would make a sparrow pie, which was always good. On Saturdays, if I wasn't wanted to clean Father's harness, I would pal up with a few bigger boys, and if it was autumn we would take a bit of bread with each of us and find a hedgehog, and dress it out, make a fire and roast him. Of course most of us would have a catapult – and good marksmen we were. This was sport. And we might get a few rabbits too, as there were plenty about in that district.

If Lewis and I wanted to get a few coppers, we would go into the woods there and pick acorns that had fallen from a big oak tree in the season, and find someone who had a pig in the sty, and we would sell them for pig food. This job was useful when we wanted a bit of spare cash. We were happy if we got twopence for the half bag of acorns – but a penny went a long way then. We might buy a ha'pennyworth of shag tobacco – it was three-ha'pence an ounce then. A little shop would give you a clay pipe if you said it was for your dad. We both smoked on the quiet.

We then moved to Suffolk, to a little place called Wenhaston, and stayed on the common there, and went to school for a while.

Still my parents insisted that we must go to school and learn to read and write – and then we needn't go any more – that was the promise. We also went to Sunday School there, at a little Wesleyan chapel on the common.

They took a collection there from the kids, I remember, the first time we went, and we hadn't any money. We didn't know we had to take a penny for the collection. We were in bad books from then on. Generous people those Wesleyans, we used to say after that, they wouldn't give a blind man a light!

So we got this persecution – even in Sunday School. And the preacher telling us how wicked it was to commit a sin and all that, what we would suffer if we did, how the heavens would descend on us, and if we committed too many sins we would be cast into a burning furnace called Hell Fire! That was the Band of Hope. Many times afterwards if we were a bit cold I would say to my brother Lewis: 'I wish we were a bit closer to that fire the minister told us about at Wenhaston!'

There was a family there with a rod tent in a little orchard just behind the little chapel I've mentioned. Their name was Picketts: one brother and three sisters. He was called Lumas, one sister was called Sally and I forget the name of the other two. We used to visit them often as boys. Lumas had a grinding barrow near the tent : his sisters would bring knives and scissors to him to sharpen. He also used to make stable lamps from glass sweet-jars. He'd fit them into a sort of carrier made of tin and he would solder a handle on them – drop a tin candlestick down it – and with a candle fitted in that was the stable lamp of those days. I don't remember who their father was but their mother was a Draper – a very beautiful woman. It was said then, although the name of Draper is heard very little today, they were real Romany people. Many of them travelled round Hitchin and Biggleswade when I was a boy, and I believe many have been settled in that area for years now.

Our next stopping place for any length of time was Tiptree Heath, near Colchester and Maldon, in Essex. There we went to school, and I remember we had a real happy time there as children. Our horses ran and grazed on the common. There were plenty of birds in the bushes too: linnets, bullfinches, chaffinches – to catch; and Father dug a real well, too. He dug down and found a spring. He sank two apple barrels down the well, one on top of the other, and we had real drinking water all the time we were there.

I remember the summer we were there. The school-children had their summer holidays for fruit picking. The biggest fruit growers were Stanley Wilkins – noted for their Tiptree jams. We went fruit picking too, like many of the other Romany families that stayed on the common then.

I remember there were a lot of Wests: Noah West, Charlie West; and David Cooper and his family and many others. The road went right through this common, and if a landau of toffs drove to Maldon, or a four-horse coach or a charabanc, we, as boys, would run alongside for a mile or more shouting for pennies and we would turn cartwheels or somersaults in return.

We had a friend who used to come on Sundays, a little midget man of those days: Lewis Spooner was his name. He was the midget that was shown for years in Bostock and Wombwell's Circus. I remember my brother Lewis was very angry when he asked him to play with him and he wouldn't: my brother wanted to fight him.

We made many friends there among the *Gaujos*, and many times we went to tea or dinner with them, and they came to us in return.

Tiptree Common was a good place for blackberries in their season, and Mother would send me and my brother Lewis to pick them: promising us all a big blackberry pudding. She would tie them up in a big pudding cloth, and our old iron boiler held eight gallons (it was on the plate: '8 galls.') so you bet some of her puddings were as big as footballs; and when she cooked she would turn them out in a big pudding bowl, and cut the lid off, and with brown sugar it was the goods. Many other Gypsy boys and girls on Tiptree has had lots of blackberry pudding made by 'Aunt Athie' – that was my mother's name.

One of my brothers was married and had one child: a girl called Emily, and more often than not we had to look after her. We would take her in a big old mail-cart. We got this job far too often, as it spoiled our play. We were sent to get blackberries one day, and of course Emily had to go with us. With the bowl in the pram we kept putting our berries in but we found it never seemed to be getting any more: Emily kept working them down her neck. After a time we thought she was asleep, but she was blue in the face and it wasn't all blackberries! We rushed her home to her mother, and they rolled Emily, and beat her back, turned her upside down and at last she parted with the blackberries. And we were never allowed to take Emily again and it pleased us too.

After this we travelled on to Gorleston, where we saw my mother's cousin Alby Smith and Madeline and their family, and at times after this travelled with them in parts of Norfolk and Suffolk. Then at Lowestoft we spent some time at Oulton Broad. There was a stopping place near called the Rock Estate; a good place for horses to graze and a lot of horse trade too. In the herring-fishing season many people needed horses for carting fish. In that season I remember old Toby Shaw was there with us – his was a very well-known family in those days. There were in the family their daughter Tilly, and many sons too: Toby, Finney, Jessie and Freddie. Toby, the eldest, used to make clothes pegs sitting under a bush, and he sat so long at this work his legs were very badly bowed, too. Old man Toby and his wife were getting on at that time, but the old woman still went out with her hawking-lorry loaded with wicker armchairs, mats, rugs and so on.

Also at Kirtley Run, near there, on the edge of the golf links as I remember, were my mother's uncle Walter Smith and his wife Matilda. She was a Lamb before she was married: a family of Romanies that has almost died out since those days. There was a big family of Lambs in Suffolk in those days: I have seen a few offspring in Norfolk a few years ago. Walter and Tilda had a big family: their two daughters Pamela and Laura, the boys' names were Adolphus, Alby, Rabie and Naughty (Naughty's proper name was Nathaniel).

We then moved around Sheringham and Cromer, and had a long stay at Fakenham. This was the last place I went to school, and from there we stayed a long time at Peterborough Stanground. This was a regular stopping place for many Travellers. From this hill we could see the hole in the cathedral which Oliver Cromwell put in with a cannonball during his marching.

From there we went to Doddington, where we stayed for a long time on the Fen. There was a lot of old Gypsy people there and there was old Jonathan Brinkley. He was called the Jawbone Breaker. He was a very good man with his hands years ago and that's how he got his name, because he did break one or two people's jaws.

He had a son named Willy who was well known in the Norfolk area, around King's Lynn and Cambridgeshire, and he used to have a grinding barrow. And the old man used to walk over from Doddington, across the Fen, on a Friday to draw his pension; it was in Lloyd George's time, five shillings a week. And Willy used to demand this five shillings off his father, against his wish of course, and Willy would walk back to the pub and used to spend this five shillings, or as much of it as he could, on drink.

And they were very poor. Had a poor old wagon. You could see holes in the side-boards of it, and when poor old Jonathan's wife was in the wagon at night-time she'd have a candle on the table, and me and my brother used to go and tease her. We'd get a bit of twig and we used to put this through the cracks of the wagon and put the candle out; and she used to stamp her feet in this old wagon and shout: 'Bloody bleeding devils in this wagon tonight! Willy! Will you give me a match to light this bloody candle!' And someone would give her a match and she'd light the candle again and we'd whip round the wagon and wipe the candle out again and she used to swear black was white that the bloody devil was in the wagon that was putting this candle out. But it was me and my brother.

Poor old girl – the last I heard of them they was going along the bank from Carter's Bridge to Ramsey and the wheel give way and buckled and collapsed and the wagon blew over into the dyke. That was the last I heard of the Brinkleys. This was about 1910.

We had a stay for a while at Grimston Common. Most of the people there had donkeys and carts to go to work in, and when we turned our horses out on the common, the donkey owners didn't like it very well because we were eating their grass. They weren't very sociable. Some were very rough, too, towards us; but they didn't have it all their own way: we had several battles, and then they set alight to the furze or gorse bushes very near our wagons and tent, but Father had his gun and fired over their heads. Some of the inhabitants of Grimston had as much intelligence as their donkeys. We stayed there for a while, and moved when we were ready.

We never felt persecuted exactly, but there was times we had to defend ourselves. I remember once we travelled to Aylesbury, Buckinghamshire. There was a common there and I remember there was some geese on that common. It was just a stopping place for the night, and we pulled on and the boys built the tent up. There were certain people that had pulled on some days previously too. And the villagers came along at night-time, the local people, and said they were going to burn our wagons.

Well, Father was never short of a gun. He was a sportsman. And he loaded his gun, and he put us children in the wagon, and when they came up that night – I quite remember – he sat on the front board of his wagon and he cropped his old gun up and he fired it above their heads and they run for their lives! I'll never forget it. They run for their lives. And next morning there were two or three old ladies and one or two old men that was partial to Romany people – they must have been because they brought some cauliflowers and lettuce, and some cabbage and carrots. They brought us a lovely feed of everything in baskets, and they were sorry for what had happened, and they said: 'If you stop you'll be alright because you've put the wind up them!'

But my father thanked them, but he said: 'We're going away. We're moving. I wouldn't have my children among a lot of villains.' And we moved on.

We travelled in Norfolk a good deal: there were many good markets there: East Dereham, Swaffham, King's Lynn and Massingham, and the country suited us both for trading and hawking.

We travelled over Suffolk too: Leiston, Saxmundham, Tunstall Common, Blaxhall Common and Knodishall Common.

I remember once we were stopping on Colfor Green at Knodishall Common, near Saxmundham, and we had our wagons at the top of the hill and it was a very severe winter, I remember, when the snow was to the tops of the bushes (furze bushes we call them – gorse bushes you do), and there was quite a lot of poor Gypsy people about: a lot of Loveridges and Tailers and Buttons and so on. And our family was a very big family at that time and Mother used to bake bread, and we used to carry it down the hill on big trays to go to a shop called Mattison's shop at the bottom of the hill. They had a bakehouse with the old-fashioned oven which they hotted up with faggots at that time. And one particular day, during this bad weather, we had sixteen or twenty loaves baked and when we carried them up to Mother at the top of the hill from the bakehouse the tragedy was these loaves had all gone *sad*, heavy, and Mother said they were too heavy for us to eat. Father said we ought to give them away to some of the poor people. Mother told us to go and give it to these poor people that had the most children that we had been playing with. And my brother Lewis and myself, quite young – I was probably ten or eleven, he would be eight or nine at that time – we did so, and we give some to a family that was newly married or had three or four little children and they called them Loveridge. And do you know, many many years past, even till about ten years ago, I was at Stanground on the hill at Peterborough, and some very good wagons was there and a curly-headed boy called Charlie Loveridge, he said to me: 'That's Gordon!' and I said: 'That's Charlie!' He said: 'I'll never forget your mother and father as long as I live. You remember when your mother's bread went sad at the bakehouse at Knodishall?' I said: 'I do well. I brought you some for your children.' He said: 'You did,' and he went on: 'It was a miracle on the Lord's side. That was absolutely necessary. We had none to eat at the time and you can see how I am now. I've never looked back!'

And that man had plenty of good-coloured horses and mares, lovely Gypsy wagons and a lovely family and had full and plenty, and had done wonderful well. That was Loveridge, and a beautiful man he was too.

And the grass was free.

The country was more or less free. There was grass on every roadside. And we could talk a policeman over. We wasn't hounded to the extent as what people are now.[14] We stopped on a crossroad, or a common, and pulled out for dinner or making a meal.

'How long are you going to stay?'

'Well, we're going to rest the horses another two hours and we're moving on, Constable.'

We would *do* that. But when it come three or four o'clock my father would look for a place with the permission of a farmer, or it would be a wide path where we wouldn't be disturbed. He used his discretion in stopping places.

You see, if you put yourself in the position, and think at that time the main source of transport was horses: and probably Father'd talk to a farmer that was a horseman, and he'd be pleased to let you pull in, and you'd perhaps see the farmer after tea having a walk round the horses. He'd be interested in one, and he'd ask the price; or have you got one for sale? Well, you could have an exchange. Father'd have a deal for anything. He'd swap for a wooden leg. And that was his life.[15]

And so we travelled freely about the country and had trade, and we boys had sport. As I grew beyond a little child there was the sport of young Gypsy boys and perhaps men too in their spare time. Well tippicat was one: a very cheap way of amusing ourselves. We'd have a piece of shaft of an ash stump sharpened at both ends and we'd lay it on a brick with the point away from us and we'd have a short stick about two foot or two foot six long and we'd hit the end of that tippicat and it would go up in the air and we'd hit it again and drive it as far as we could. And then we'd run and see in how many strides you could get to it, and the winner would get a bit of money – cigarettes or money. That was one amusement. And a hop, skip and a jump. Or three rising jumps. Or a running long jump, that was another sport. Simple, nice games like that. Or vaulting over a gate: some could run and jump over a five-barred gate; some could only vault over it, putting one hand on. And then walk along the gate and those who could walk along it like a tight-rope – to beat him you'd have to hop along it on one foot.

There was always boxing. Just with your flat hands. Just a frame-up and give us a spar with your flat hands, or wrap some rag round your hands so we wouldn't hurt each other. That sort of business – and we loved that, we loved that.

And there was always the poaching. Bit of coursing, cata-pults; going out Christmas-time or February, when the cold weather was on, blackbirds and thrushes in the bottom of a hedge. We'd go one each side and kill birds and fetch them home or even stop and light a fire and roast one or two. Take a bit of bread with us. That was a day's sport for an innocent boy. It was the only sport we had. We made our own – it was a day out for us.

The older men used to go out at the right time of the year in winter-time and go hedgehogging and they'd find hedge-hogs and fetch them home and probably stop on the road and have one – they'd call that a day's sport. And they would be cooked when they got home on a spit. They was cooked the right way: shaved and singed and split down the back like a kipper, opened out and cleaned and washed and the old Gypsy people, my people, we liked hedgehog – we had a few now and again at the right time of year. January and February when they was empty they would be opened out, laid in salt and water, and they would be put on a spit the next day stuck in the ground by a stick fire, and you basted it with the fat that run off and it was very nice. But some people liked boiled hedgehog but we never did fancy it. We always liked roast hedgehog. It's very dainty. Very nice. Some people say it tastes like pheasant, or some people say it tastes like venison, roasted venison. But I think it tastes of game. It's very, very nice I think. I haven't had one for two winters now. I did intend to have one. I intended to find one this winter and have it roasted and bring Dick Wade to supper. Bit of a joke of me. I said: 'One of these days, when the water takes up and the hedges are a bit drier and I can walk about I'll find one and I will cook it and I'll invite Dick to come and have a do with me!'[16]

And snails: I still like them, I like them at the right time of the year, the back-end, when they've clustered up together and they've laid perhaps in the bottom of a nice old stump of a tree, or a whitethorn stump. If they are a good sample and big enough and clean and a clump of snails all stuck together, I like to wash them and put them in boiling water and strain the water off them; and I like to open them, eat them with a skewer or a nail or a fork. And dipped in salt, with some bread, some good bread and butter and some strong tea, I like them, when I can find them.

But there's not many stumps of trees now in Lincolnshire. But if you get further up Spilsby way I've found them in the stump of an ash tree. You'll find them in a good wall, an old-fashioned wall, you'll find them in the split of a wall. I can go and find them if I want to, but none of my family eat them now.

I don't think – I don't think there's any Romany, any Gypsy articles left in these people today. I don't think they look for hedgehogs; I don't think they look for a rabbit –

there's a lot of people keeps a dog and there's a lot got good dogs, but there's a lot of Gypsy people don't think about keeping a dog to go coursing with now. They buy what they want.

But with us it was always the dog. If you had a dog – any kind of a lurcher dog that could hunt and kill and carry – it was the mainstay for the menu of the table. A good dog was absolutely priceless, you wouldn't sell it under any consideration. It was one of the family. A man needn't walk about a field with a dog: he could put the dog over a gate and it'd go on the field and kill something and bring it back and the man would never trespass.

I'm going back to my boyhood days, especially in Essex, Suffolk and Norfolk. The older Gypsy people, they was hot on pheasant's eggs and partridge's eggs in the restricted areas. That was well known for some of my father's people, and my mother's people, that would travel from Thetford to Brandon to Bury St Edmunds and back again. The old womenfolk at the time they kept pockets in their petticoats; and one of them would be walking in a covert or a wood, and she wouldn't be suspected by a keeper of poaching: the man would pay respect and turn his head away and probably think that the lady went into that wood to relieve herself. And she would pick up the pheasant's and partridge's eggs and she would put them in her petticoat pockets, and they could carry several.

And it was known that one of my father's people, a woman, had a cat that used to go and find these eggs in the coverts for her, and she used to pick them up and they were put in the false bottom of the caravan or old wagon. It was known in my father's time there was a false bottom kept in a cart or wagon to roll these eggs in, and they could be taken to different places where they could be sold even in those days for a shilling each to gentry to rear them and so on.

But in my day in Essex and Suffolk and Norfolk, of course, pheasants was very tame and you could sit on your cart and cut the head off one with a whip. They wouldn't move out of your road: they were hand-fed birds and we had plenty of those. And there was plenty of times we had twenty partridge's or pheasant's eggs for breakfast. Father would restrict us and told us we had no right to do it, but at that time we was thinking: What right, what right has that one man over that estate? What right has he got to have all those lovely things in life and we can't even have a pheasant's egg? But there was several of my father's people has been known to be heavily fined and imprisoned for taking a swede out of a field, a turnip out of a field in Suffolk. It was persecution again. It seemed all wrong why one man should have all the lovely things of life and we can't have an egg. We travel about, we can't keep pheasants, we can't keep chickens: what was wrong if we went to a farm? There was no hen-coops in those days, the hens would lay at the bottom of hedges along the roadside; and if we could find a nest of eggs we'd have some, I know I would. It was against my father's wishes but he didn't know everything you see. We thought it: why should those people be covetous over what they owned? They didn't want anybody: they wired you in and they wired you out; there were locks on gates; there were keepers to keep you out; there was 'trespassers will be prosecuted' on common land that was self-claimed by these people – it was joined on to what they had already bought. And that was the feeling I think of most Gypsy people in those days.

I don't say a Gypsy man would go through a gate to have a chicken, but it has been known for a chicken to ramble along the side of a road; it has been known for a man to chop one up with a whip and then puts its head under a cart wheel. If it was found it had been run over: kind of an excuse – it's a lame excuse I know but it did happen – it had happened with me.

Another amusement: the boys used to like cock-fighting. It's in a lot of the boys' feelings now, and I still think in various parts of the country that cock-fighting is done today – I honestly believe that. I know in Leeds there was cock-fighting – I've been to a cock-fight in Leeds – but it's many years ago, 'twenty-one or 'twenty-two. There was cock-fighting in a old disused mill, till they got carved up by the police. Plenty of the Welsh Travelling people used to carry fighting cocks about with them, game cocks; they liked the game cock, they liked that breed. They trimmed the combs and all like that and they had sport together. Even kids, Travelling kids, even today you see them with bantams and all like that. And when they meet they let the chickens loose and have a cock-fight. Well, when the boys are assembled together you can't stop the bantam cockerels from having a fight, can you? We've had them here in this yard when they've fought, they've run all round this yard, underneath vehicles, but they've been their own blood-brothers you know. I had several of the silver spurs that was put on cock-erels and they're very valuable if you can find them. I had three or four of them at one time as relics, but I was never able to keep them.

We were very, very healthy – we never ailed, or went to the doctor. We always had our own remedies for things.

We never was without comfrey ointment.

There's a blue flower and a white flower, called male and female. And we believed that ointment from the male flower was good with the female and vice versa. But my mother used to make an ointment from this comfrey. She used to get it both male and female, and cut it very short, like a salad, and put it in the boiler, and she used to find a pork butcher with some fresh leaf lard and she used to cut that up in small pieces to mix with that short salad comfrey – and we used to stew this leaf lard and this comfrey. Now when it had sim-mered for a long, long time and all the fat had gone out of the leaf lard she would put it through a fine piece of muslin or a colander and strain it and put it in jars – old stone jam jars at that time – and we used to use it for burns, cuts on children, anything like a scald, or if we had a cut on a horse, got cut on barbed wire. We was great believers in comfrey.

Or we'd get elderberries, the leaves, the young shoots off the top of the leaves, where they spread. We would soak them in hot water. That would wither them to a certain extent to make it look like a vegetable, and we would put them all round a horse's leg, a lame horse, and we would get a piece of tent blanket and make it into a bandage and bandage it, and it would sweat it, it would sweat that leg down. It would come up again in time but continue bandaging like that for, say, three or four days you could bet that leg would be normal for a long time. Until it was neglected again. It was a great help.

We're great believers in mandrake, too. I could trace a mandrake in any old-fashioned part where there's a bank or an old-fashioned bit of hedge, and I could follow the line and I could tell you where that mandrake was, and I could either step ten yards to the right of that, or ten yards to the left, and I could guarantee that I could find the fellow-mate to that mandrake. We used to dig them up, and they are just made like human beings, not so perfect, but they've got arms and legs, body just the same as a male or female – some more perfect than others but they're there. You can discern just the parts of the natural body of male and females. Some of them are very old. It takes years for one to come to maturity.

I remember, after I grew up, digging one out in my mother-in-law's garden in Spilsby in Lincolnshire. It took me four or five evenings' work to dig round it carefully, it was so big. And I took my time in digging it out, and when I got almost to the bottom I'd dug four foot or more down. I thought I could pull one of these legs up and get it out perfect – one leg was shorter than the other.

And, you may find it hard to believe, but when I pulled it out it did groan. It would put the wind up a man to hear what I did. It did groan. For the mandrake is a human herb and if you disfigure them, if you hurt them in any way, they will groan.

The big one will weigh a stone, a stone and a half. But they're like parsnip content, and you'd dry them off, hang them up and let them dry and they'd go tough, withered and hard; and in those past years we used to grind a bit on a nutmeg grater and put it in a bran mash for a horse once a week. You see it was good for the blood. It would make a horse's coat look silky, if you was getting one ready, if you kept a nice horse. It would refine the coat.

And we used to sell the rest to herbalist chemists, and we used to sell pieces: people would buy it and put a piece in a wine glass like a piece of lemon and they'd drink it. It would be good for the blood.

Many years ago one of my brothers, he was bad with his chest, and we believed that when we put this mandrake through the nutmeg grater, put it in a saucepan and made tea of it, boiled and simmered it away – it's very bitter you understand – and mixed it with boiled sugar and he took a wine-glass full of it, he had it every morning, we believed that it *eased* my brother (he's since died). It eased my brother more than all the doctor's medicine he was supplied with. We was great believers in mandrake.

≈§ 4 ≈

The Mission Tent

WELL the time came when my father was given the Gypsy Mission tent. John Wesley Baker finished with it. Somehow his connections with the Free Trade Hall at Manchester which was the head of the Gypsy Mission at that time finished. They finished with Baker. He wasn't a man that could move like my father. And I think he lost his speeches among the Gypsy people. At least we thought so. And my father took over the tent and the collapsible seats and the coconut mat that went on the floor, and we had that tent – and of course we had the wagon that John Wesley Baker had at that time which was another wagon that was made at Tongs of Manchester, a wagon with three doors where you could walk right through. It was a gorgeous wagon. It was made of mahogany panels and inside was mahogany and canary wood and it had double shafts too and it weighed over three ton. It wanted two horses, two big horses, to go in it. And this wagon, my father and I brought it from the Gypsy Mission at Manchester and then my father started to run the Gypsy Mission tent, and we built this tent at Tiptree, in Essex, on Tiptree Common, near Colchester, and we stayed there for two years or more.

My mother and father used to take it in turns preaching. My sister Laura used to play the harmonium. She was a wonderful singer at that time and the hymn books that was by the Gypsy Mission had all the good old-time hymns and of course us smaller children was made to attend that service every Thursday for a meeting. Sundays they'd have a morning service and we used to get the Gypsy people to come, and a lot of the village people used to come along, and Father used to give a sermon as well as he could, and Mother was a God-fearing woman and we had a lot of converts through Mother and Father: most of them passed on now.

The Mission Tent

And then we moved the tent to a place near Southend, the Bohemia Estate. And I went to school there. We had the mission tent there and I remember Gypsy Rodney Smith, the evangelist, come to stay with us and I was his favourite boy and my sister insisted on me sleeping with him because we let him have our big old wagon to sleep in because he was a prominent sort of character. My father was a relation of Gypsy Rodney Smith's wife, distant relation. Of course he used to give missions all over the country.

Then we moved on to Cambridgeshire. We came on Doddington, and I remember my people was there for four years and there was a lot of Gypsy people used to stop on the common at that time. Most of them working on the land or something: potato picking – or strawberry picking, and they say that at both sides of the road there was seven hundred acres of common land and we used to turn our horses out and forget them. And my father used to buy and sell a horse – and we had our mission tent there. My father had to have a deal with a horse still, couldn't help it. He'd more or less toe the line though, and have an honest trade with the man and give the man a fair trial with the horse. He bought something that was reliable, and if it didn't turn out right he would take it back and satisfy the man another way.

My father and mother was paid for the mission work by a monthly cheque. Every month I remember a cheque used to come from the Free Trade Hall at Manchester – I believe it was only a little. It was about eight pounds a month. But we did rely on collection to keep the tent in repair, to buy coke and keep it heated, and paraffin oil. We had four hanging lamps in it for lights. And there was paint. And that was the last place my father and mother had the Gypsy Mission tent. I think it was then Gypsy Rodney Smith left England for his evangelistic work in America, when both in my opinion, as a boy, and in my father's opinion, he deserted his race of people. As a great man, as we thought he was at that time, we thought it was a terrible thing for him to go to America and preach the gospel among a different class of people.

And we more or less disinherited him in our opinions.

And he went to America and made vast lots in America; and I remember, about 1937, I was on Cambridge Common at the Midsummer Fair, and he did keep a house in Cambridge, and he came over with his secretary – I remember he had a blonde secretary, and he was looking for Gypsy people, inquiring about the Boswells and so on.

Someone directed him to me and he said: 'I'm Rodney Smith.'

I said: 'I'm Gordon Boswell.' I said: 'I'm the boy that used to sleep with you at Southend.'

'Where's your mother and father?'

'They're at Skegness. And I think it's your duty to go and see them.'

But he couldn't find time.

I said: 'That's right!' and I spoke my mind to him, because I didn't care for him or anybody else. At the time I had no particular wealth. I had my home and my wife and two or three children. And I said to him: 'You know you've done a terrible thing after you was uplifted by the name of Gypsy. You were a leader among poor people, and you was needed and your teaching and education. You suddenly picked your stakes up and you went to America and you massed a great fortune over there. In our estimation you made a fortune. You've come back for a holiday. And the Gypsy people that was old enough to know what you was doing at the time – even your close relations like there was at Eastwood – they thought it was a shameful thing. You must have been money-crazy to do it. You should have been the very man that might have been a turning-point in the Gypsies' lives by bringing up with that education that you have got some of it. And I believe you and my father and mother with their good way of living could have been the turning-point among a lot of Gypsies to bring them on a level with somebody else. But you went to America, you amassed a fortune and evidently you'll probably marry this young lady.'

And he did, and he died. And no doubt about it: she's got all he left behind.

But he was shocked to think that there was a Gypsy boy or a man could ever tell him off so short in my humble way, and I said: 'I shall tell my father that you was in Cambridge when I see him. And I know what he'll think, and I know what he will say, because I know my father better than you do. My poor father's a staunch man. And when I go back to Skegness and I see my father I'll tell him I've seen Rodney Smith. And I know his words that he will say.'

And he said: 'What are they?'

'He'll say: "Ha! What about him? He's bit the hand that's fed him, and he's gone over there for wealth." And Rodney – *Uncle* Rodney, you're far older than me – I don't think you and my father liked each other too well, did you? He was pulling one way and you was pulling the other. You wanted to go high, you went to people with education that didn't need you. It was the people that you left that needed you!'

And he walked out of my trailer and he said: 'God bless you.'

I said: 'He will. He will bless me and my people too. And I shall do all that's in my power to assist them and try and bring them on a level, in my humble way. I'm a man of the world – I'm not a God-fearing man but I respect God.' And that's the last I saw of him.

When the Gypsy Mission was finished, my father and mother was instructed to take anything they wanted. Because it was only a tent and this wagon. Probably the Gypsy Mission couldn't afford to finance another tent. There were the tarpaulin sheets – there were the bundles of rods – and when we moved, you see, we couldn't remove this tent by horse vehicles – we used to put it on goods trains in trucks. There was two or three truck-loads of this business, this tent. The wagon went by road, of course, because we had the horses to pull it. We had two big wagons and the boys' wagon as well. We had a roadful of stuff at that time. And then it gradually collapsed. My father and mother finished with it in about 1912, and of course there was the threat of war in 1914 and they travelled on with the wagons to Skegness.

5

The Boy becomes a Man

I LEFT home at the age of twelve years.

I had ninepence in a mustard tin, that I'd saved up.

But it was because of this school – this national school I was going to at the time. At that time I was a very good drawer: animals, birds, anything. And there was a competition among the boys and girls for the best drawing of an animal.

And when the authorities come round to judge, these particular drawings of mine were picked out as the best of them. And I remember old Smith, the schoolmaster – he was a severe old man – he used to knock us about and cane us for nothing, make us stand with great big slates on our heads (it was the time when they changed from slates to copy books) and we'd have to stand with seven or eight slates on our heads and he'd slap you up the ear-hole and the slates would slide.

And I remember him saying to these two or three people when they was about to bring me out for this prize: 'Oh – he's a Gypsy boy! He's not saying here long.'

And there was this banner to be presented.

It was a velvet thing with a banner on it, and it was supposed to hang in the school. And he said: 'If he wins he can't take the banner out of the school.'

So they gave it to the second best.

It hurt me. I was Gypsy again, you see. It was another bit of persecution. And I cried when I got home and I said: 'I will never go to that school again.' And I ran away.

Two brothers were travelling down Lowestoft way with their hawking-lorry, because our family was so big that they had to branch off and get what they could; and I walked from Doddington to Lowestoft.[17] I didn't tell my mother and father. I made my way to Lowestoft, and I stuck with those brothers for a time. And it comes springtime and I left them, and went back to Doddington to find my people, and they wasn't there.

And I heard talk of my friend Rodney Brinkley that used to stop at Doddington – he was working in a season with old Jimmy Grange that had the bathing-machines on the beach at Hunstanton – and I'd heard him say what good times he had, and what good tips; and Rodney was my pal, and it was just Easter-time, and I thought: Well I'll walk and walk and I'll go to Rodney. I wouldn't turn my back and give up. I was at that time about twelve and a half years old.

And I smoked at that time, and Woodbines were a penny, and I smoked and bought buns, and I remember when I got to King's Lynn, and I was going on the old Hunstanton Road, tired, and an old man gave me a lift in a tumble cart. And he said: 'Where are you going?'

'I'm going to my uncle at Hunstanton.'

'Who's your uncle?'

'Old Jimmy Grange.' I'd heard Rodney talk about old Jimmy Grange, and I didn't want this man to copper on me and send me back and report me.

Anyway, I put myself over alright, and rode as far as I could. Glad to get off his cart – he was asking too many questions. And I went marching on.

But I didn't know where Rodney Brinkley was. It was getting late at night and I'd spent my money: every penny of it – and I didn't know where to go. I walked down to the beach, and I saw a few bathing-machines and I wandered up that beach towards Heacham, and I was very hungry: I ate some mussels off the breakwater stumps. I always had a knife, because that was the first thing my father ever bought me, was a knife. And I sat down and opened these mussels, the biggest ones on the breakwater, and I had a feed of mussels.

And I walked farther up that beach, getting dark, and I saw more bathing-machines: they'd been stored away from the sea for the winter months, you see, and well, I thought to myself, when it gets a bit darker I'll hide myself in one of these old bathing-machines and lay down. And I did. I opened one of these doors and lay down on a seat, and I wasn't long falling asleep and I had a very sound sleep.

In the morning I intended to get up and go down to the beach and wash my face and so on, but before I did get up I was awakened by a noise, and I listened, a bit nervous, and I could hear some chains rattling. And I opened this door, got it ajar and looked through, and I saw someone putting a collar and traces on an old black mare.

And all in a second I could see that it was Rodney! The back of him – I knew him in a minute because he was a very keen boy in having a coachman's melton coat made by a tailor and cut into an ordinary coat. And his cord trousers with the raised seams round the bottom. I could see the back of Rodney, it was my old pal Rodney! He'd be about three or four years older than me. Rodney – he's dead now.

And when I shouted 'Rodney!' I give him the shock of his life! He'd frightened me and I'd frightened him.

He said: 'Whatever are you doing here?'

'I've come to find you. You'll have to do something for me.'

'Where have you come from?'

'Doddington.'

'Have you had anything to eat?'

'I haven't had much to eat for two days. Not since I left King's Lynn.'

So he put the bridle on this mare, this old black mare. And he jumped up on this mare, put his foot in the loop of the chain and jumped on, and I swung up behind him, and away we went! Down to the beach, where the few bathing-machines were to be worked, you see, with a few of the visitors that had come early, and there was a little corner café and he sat me down and I had eggs, bacon, toast, tea, cigarettes. And you could get bacon and eggs for fourpence at that time, you know. He spent about eightpence or tenpence on me and I'm alright. I feel a lot better.

He was living in one of these bathing-machines: using it as a wagon, until the season come on.

'Now,' he said, 'I've got to go to the bathing-machines, because old Mrs Grange and Jimmy Grange will be down.'

It wasn't quite Easter, and Rodney's working these few bathing-machines with early bathers: this old black mare pulling the bathing-machines out to sea. Taking a bit of money. And then old Jimmy Grange come and Rodney told him who I was and what I'd come for.

Jimmy Grange said: 'Well you'll have to hang about a bit. We'll do what we can for you, before the season starts – we'll have an extra horse soon.'

Because it was a two-horse job you see. We had about twenty or thirty bathing-machines. I earned a few shillings painting and that until the season started, and then old Jimmy Grange give me an old greasy-legged mare. She was broken-backed, and she would go forward but she wouldn't go back, and she had a greasy leg. And I worked those bathing-machines that summer.

Well, me and Rodney at that time, we were two wide boys, you know.

We used to send to Cambridge – to Lees of Cambridge – for some watches with romping horses on them – because they were one-and-ninepence a time. We used to send for a dozen of these, and a few dud brass chains and white metal chains, and we used to go to a pub called The Cows, or The Cowshed – it was a wooden building – and we'd sell a few of these watches, and perhaps a chain, and I used to play the mouth-organ and Rodney would step-dance.[18] He was a good step-dancer but he was all in one position you know; he would step-dance and I would play little hornpipes and jigs for him. It wasn't much of a do but it amused them at the time and we was well-liked two lads, you know. We used to sell a watch or two to them, and a bob or two that way, and of course the bathing-machines, and it was a happy life.

I was a bit of a villain, and Rodney was no angel, and at that time there was no mini-skirts about and no woman would ever show her ankles. And probably you'd get a courting couple that was allowed to come from home to the seaside, and they'd have a bathe for the first time, and the boy would try to get his girl in to have a bathe, and we'd try to fix them up with a double compartment machine and we'd say: 'It's quite alright – there are two compartments – you are quite alright.'

All the doors had lock and bolt of course. And we'd get the costumes and charge them sixpence each, and put the boy in one and the girl in the other you see – and perhaps the tide would be out, and Rodney would wink at me. And we'd give them a rough journey over the stones. And perhaps she'd be undressing, and the boy would be undressing, and all the boards would whip and wobble and, bang! the doors had sprung open and you'd hear the girl scream! And probably the boy'd see more of the girl than he ever did of his sister in his life! Then when we'd pull them back it was: 'Enjoy your bathe, Sir?' Yes, well if he did enjoy it, if that boy did enjoy it, and sometimes you know what might happen, he'd give us a tip. And perhaps he'd give us sixpence. 'Is *that* all you're going to give – for the experience you've had? Eh! Drop it in a bit heavier than that!' And we'd get a shilling.

Then you know, if it was a real hot day, we might get a fat woman, a very fat woman. She'd want to bathe, but she'd never been used to the water. We'd say to her husband: 'It's quite alright! You can have a double bathing-machine, Sir, and you can look after your wife. We'll give you a rope to put round her waist.'

Well we'd go and find a costume, and it was like red duck you know, what they make wagon sheets out of now. Red duck, or blue. There was all frills round the bottom with elastic in, and frills round the sleeves and white braid round the neck. All buttoned up tight. But we'd get a kind of costume that was a bit weak at the stitches, because old Mother Grange used to keep a sewing-machine in a bathing-machine to mend these costumes, because the salt water used to rot the cotton, you see. Well we'd judge the size of this fat woman, we'd find a costume that'd be a tight squeeze for her, and she'd get this costume on and we'd just pull this machine out into about two or three feet of water, and we'd have this rope round her, and the husband would stand on the front and she'd bob up and down.

Well it was a long time before this costume got really wet, you know, because it was like canvas; but all the time she was bobbing up and down this water was popping up her legs, inside this canvas, and it was gradually coming up her waist, and suddenly her husband would say: 'Get down! Get down in the water! Get up to your neck!'

Well when she did this she was like a balloon you see – full of water. Her head would go down in the water and her legs would come up. Her husband would pull on this rope, and get her out, and shout: 'What can we do with this? How can we get the water out?'

'Well there's only one thing to do, Sir. I shall have to let the water out of the bottom.'

Well I used to pull my knife out, and cut the elastic at the bottom of both legs.

'Oh don't touch my legs! Don't touch my legs!'

'It's quite alright! It's quite alright! It will have to be done!'

Or it might be a man with his girl friend – and we could see what they was at.

The man would probably wink at us, and we'd pull that bathing-machine out on its own. And of course we would expect a tip, if he was a decent fellow at all. Or perhaps he'd give us sixpence, and we'd say: 'What – for all that length of time! Surely – you've enjoyed yourself! Drop it in a bit heavy! When you come again I'm not going to use my horse to pull you all the way out *there* for your convenience!'

So we'd get a shilling.

And of course we had the élite of the country, that used to come to the seaside.

I remember there was Admiral Truebridge, from Norwich. A lovely family of people. And the Gurneys, the banking people of Norwich. They used to stay in a house on the front, and there was a lovely lot of girls, and they used to bathe and we used to race with these two old horses and the bathing-machines and the one that used to win would get a shilling.

But I remember we was galloping them back one day and they had a French poodle, a very valuable dog – it was the first one I'd ever seen in my life. And we was galloping them back and this poodle kept barking at the nose of my horse, and then the horse got it under its feet and the wheel ran over it and killed it. And it was like the loss of a child. And I got a box, and made a coffin, and we buried it in the garden of the house they rented, and we put a stone there, and a cross, and we had the name painted, and we got all different types of shells off the beach to put around it, to make the girls happy.

And they used to bring Rodney and me lovely sandwiches: as thin as razor blades with little bits of ham and pastry. The best we'd ever had in our lives. Lovely. And bottles of ginger beer, and tea and something. They were beautiful girls, and they thought a lot of Rodney and me because we obliged them with the bathing-machines.

That first season I was there, old Jimmy Grange got some ponies on the beach, and he had a dappled-grey and I fancied it, and I bought this dapple-grey pony for four pounds. Beautiful pony it was. Wasn't very good in harness, though. And Rodney bought the old black mare with the greasy heel; but with going in that amount of salt water it would come up perfect, and we douched it, and it was a bonny little mare and this mare only cost him about four pounds ten. So we were two horse-owners around there. And I remember we went and found an old cart for seven shillings, and an old set of harness, and we left Hunstanton and started travelling together, and we got on the road for King's Lynn.

Rodney sold his mare for a profit in King's Lynn market, and I swapped my pony for a cheaper pony and drawed a bit of money, and we sold the cart, so we was without anything at the time, but later in the day we bought another pony, and we put it in a public house yard at King's Lynn. And we put some straw in the next standing, and we slept in the standing, in the stable.

I was thirteen then. And the next year I promised to go back to old Jimmy Grange but I didn't. I went off on my own, travelling up and down, and I stayed with my brother that winter at Wisbech St Mary's, and he was breaking some horses in – some flea-bitten greys belonging to John Russel, of Wisbech St Mary's, and I helped him break these horses.

But I couldn't stick it. I felt the ramble on me again. I went back to Hunstanton, but I couldn't find Rodney, so I got a job at Calaby's Riding Stables. They were funeral proprietors, coal merchants: everything. And they had a big string of horses, and used to drive a coach four-in-hand as the season went on: every Thursday and Sunday. These four horses on the coach used to drive to Old Hunstanton, Brancaster Bay, Holkham and on to Sandringham Grounds, and then get a fresh relay of horses at Sandringham and come home.

I could tackle the horses. I got so I could tackle up these horses, and drive too, and I knew the different types of horses that was going on because the horses was picked for it, of course. Two special horses for the pole – especially the wheelers, the nearside ones; anything could go on the off-side because it didn't make no difference: they could be a bouncer or a kicker. He'd have to come – have to follow the other horses. And there was times when we had fresh horses on the outside and I used to have to jump down and hold their heads, because there was a coachful of people.

Calaby's had, oh, one of the best well-known hackney stallions there was in England at that time. It was a horse called Leopard, and it was shown all over the country. And I used to help with some of the two-year-olds, and help break them in the ring and so on with Horace Calaby. And then probably there'd be some ladies want to ride side-saddle, and gentlemen with them, and they had to have somebody to follow them. And perhaps I'd have the job of following the ladies and gentlemen to Old Hunstanton and mind their horses while they had a drink or something of the kind, and it was another place to get tips.

Old Jimmy Grange had a field at Hunstanton, very close to the shore, and Fossett's Circus came to this field, and of course it was time then to finish with the riding school, and I used to talk to these circus boys, and they had a lot of ponies and the like, and I thought to myself I might get a job with this circus.

And I went with the circus. But I didn't stop long. I didn't like the life. I liked the work – I was a pony-boy, washing ponies for them, getting them ready for the ring, cleaning tackle in the daytime, sleeping under a lorry or in the circus tent, anywhere you could find. But they had a lot of casual labour, and they'd perhaps be boiling a sheep's head in a bucket, to eat, and then be boiling their shirt in the same bucket later on, and that wasn't my way of life.[19] I followed them to King's Lynn and then to Swaffham, and I suddenly disappeared. I'd had enough. I loved the animals, the beautiful ponies and all like that. But I couldn't stand the dirt.

But the real circus people, they are Travelling people. They was like Gypsy people, I'm certain of that – a black strain of people. A Gypsy boy or man fitted in, because they was wagon people, and they was quite at home in their wagons, they never lived in anything else. You know: the Fossetts and the Pinders, all circus people. They would speak plain English – do you understand me? – it was either plain English or if they wanted to say anything to you on the side they'd say it in Romany.[20] And of course I was always that type of boy could throw a Romany word or two out there – to see what they was. And that made me welcome.

I think if I'd stopped with the circus I would probably have been my own master in time, because I always fancied it. But probably I was dreaming. Imagination. But it's what boys used to think about at that time, for improvement in life. I would have loved to have been a circus man, because I was a very good rider. I could vault over anything, and I was probably a very suitable man. But of course I left.

My people then was at Peterborough for a time, at Standground, and I went back to them for a week or two. But then I went back Norfolk way, and travelling by myself again.

I went to King's Lynn market and bought a donkey.

There was little Johnnie Wilkinson, a little miniature man, and he had a drove of donkeys every week there. I bought one for thirteen shillings, a two-year-old donkey, and I was marching him home. I had a new suit of clothes on – little tight trousers, blue serge – and I was marching him over the bridges, and I thought I could ride anything so I said: 'I'll ride you!', and when I got him on a lonely road I jumped on his back. Well, he was going along quite comfortable, but it wasn't long before he put his head down between his legs and I was over! And my trousers were so tight – it was 'pencil-cases' in them days or 'drain-pipe trousers' we called them – I busted both knees of my trousers and I cried to myself about my suit because it was the first time I'd had it on! I remember that with my temper I bit a piece out of the donkey's ear!

And when I got to Wisbech I went down to North Street; and all the dealing men used to come and stand outside the picture palace, assemble there, you know. And I would listen to them, and so on. And there was one fellow called Austin Willy, a nice fellow, and he used to buy a good cart-horse. And he said: 'Now then Darkie' – he used to call me Darkie – 'where have you been today?'

'I've bought a donkey at King's Lynn.'

'What are you going to do with it?'

'I'm going out tatting.'

'Oh well. That's alright. What sort of donkey have you got? If you want it to go fast you want to dock it.'

But I never docked my black donkey. But it was a nice little donkey. I hadn't got a cart, and I hadn't got any donkey harness, but I borrowed some donkey harness and there was an old man in Wisbech that used to lend hand-carts out for fourpence a week, and I borrowed one of these carts, and put a pair of shafts on it, and I went out tatting.[21]

And Austin Willy said: 'If you want to make your donkey go fast, get a bit of sand and put it down one of its ear-holes. It won't be long before you get a bit of speed, my son.'

Well I took this for granted.

Anyway, I got to Wisbech St Mary, and this donkey knocked himself up for me trying to do too much of it and he lay down in harness. There were gravel roads at that time, and I got a bit of grit from the side of the road, and pulled the biggest stones from it, and I dropped it down this donkey's ear. And he shook his head, and he didn't give me time to grab hold of the reins to stop this donkey, and away he went, and he turned into the first gateway and smashed old Johnnie's cart to pieces! And it wasn't mine, and I couldn't afford to replace it, and the poor cart was broke in pieces!

I led my donkey home.

It was days before I dared to tell old Johnnie, and, oh, it was months before I had enough money to pay for his cart and, the old sod, he charged me two pounds ten for my cart. He used to make them himself.

Of course, at Wisbech, we spent fair times there.

I think Wisbech was the first tuition of me really in the scrap business.

Because there's a very rich firm at Wisbech, and was many years ago, and it's still standing today: Friends of Wisbech. And the original father of that firm was called Mush Friend.[22]

And his old lady used to sit down in her shed, with her black apron on and a pocketful of coppers, and she used to buy jam-jars, pound jam-jars two for a penny, two-pound jars two for three ha'pence and so on. And I heard that some of the tatting boys, like they do in other places, could go to old Mother Friend and say: 'Give us a kick-off for the day! Half a quid or a dollar!'

And I got another cart, and I went to old Mush Friend, and they liked me, and they said: 'What do you want this morning?'

'I want a bit of money to go on with.'

'How much do you want?'

'Five shillings, Mr Friend.'

And he'd say to his wife: 'Darkie wants five shillings. Can't you do with half-a-crown, my son?'

'No. I'll have five bob. I'm going out where I think I can get a fair bit of stuff.'

And they'd mess me about, and in the finish they

intended to lend me five shillings. And I had to go out and get a bit of brass, and a little bit of iron – somebody would break a stove up – a few rabbit skins – anything I could load up.

And I would come and weigh the stuff in at old Mrs Friend and perhaps draw seven or eight shillings for that load. Or eight or nine shillings or whatever it come to.

Perhaps I'd cop a feather-bed, and that was good because feather-beds was selling at that time. A feather-bed at that time would make ten or twelve shillings and if I could cop a feather-bed that was a good day's work on top of this load of scrap. And I'd perhaps go away and I'd say this is alright: I've earned five or six shillings. And I'd buy a bit of corn you see, fourpence a stone, a bit of mixed corn for your donkey or your little pony. And I had a bit of a shed to put it in and we was happy! Happy as the birds in the air!

Then we'd go to the theatre, me and my pal Frank Gibson, we'd go to the Hippodrome, go up in the gods for twopence. And perhaps come outside and have a basin of peas. There was a woman used to have a stall outside with some hot peas. Or we'd go to the fish and chip shop and sit down and have fish and chips. We used to call it 'ride one and lead one'. Fish and chips for a penny-ha'penny. And they used to sell a bottle of stout for twopence if you wanted it, or a cup of tea for a ha'penny and a slice of bread for a ha'penny at that time.

And that's how we used to live: and some really good turns at the Hippodrome, you know. They was really happy times. I thought they was beautiful times.

I was only a kid, but I was having a *try*, and I was trying to make myself into a man, and the sooner I got into the man the better and I mixed with men's company you know.

And there was other comical lads besides me in Wisbech at that time. There was one – he's dead now – Chitty Crickmore. Well I went to Downham Wednesday Fair which was a good fair that time, and Chitty had a big old bouncing mare and a big old square cart and we drove to Downham Wednesday Fair and he bought a little Shetland pony. I think it was two pounds. And I bought a big old donkey with a lot of hair on it, and I set off with the Shetland pony and the donkey back to Wisbech. And we got these things home, but the black and white pony died that night.

And when his wife come out we was standing outside this picture palace. His wife said: 'Chitty?'

'What, my dear?'

'You'd better come quick – the pony is dead!'

'Oh well,' he said, 'we can't do any more with it now, Missus. It's not above seventy guineas lost.'

He was a real game lad! It cost two pounds.

At that time me and Chitty used to go out with a clipping machine and we used to clip people's horses out, you know – bakers' cobs and that sort. Take the top off and leave the legs for seven-and-six you know. They'd bring us a pot of tea. Perhaps it'd be on a Sunday morning, and we'd perhaps have three or four clients like that, and go and have half a day's clipping and we'd go on a pound – that was half a quid each, you know. And perhaps one of them men would give you an order for a little set of harness. Well, we'd come down to somebody who had a set of harness to sell, and they'd sell it to us for thirty bob or thirty-five bob, and at that time a set of old pony harness could perhaps sell for two pounds.

It was all that. There was ways and means of getting a living – if you kept going. That was it: never give up.

We *couldn't* give up. How could we? We had nobody to lean on. Only ourselves, in those days. We *had* to have a go! Boys was men. And if you had any intelligence about you, you was respected by men: they liked a good boy, we'd give 'em a bit of a go.

'We'll have a deal with him because I think he'll make himself into a man!'

And perhaps the man who was thinking that or doing that for you had been a pioneer himself – he'd started from nothing and he'd got somewhere. So he'd give another young boy the same chance even if it was only the matter of a shilling to benefit that boy. He liked doing it; that was the feeling. But there is not that feeling today. There isn't those boys looking for that livelihood – they're waited on hand

and foot, aren't they? They're ornaments, they're not men at all. And I wouldn't like to live in the next generation myself. I don't want to. I want to go to sleep.

I've picked strawberries at a farthing a pound. Got up at three o'clock in the morning and picked till seven to get the early market. Or perhaps on a farm you'd have to pick at four o'clock at night and pick till dark. But a farthing a pound and today they are demanding fourpence or fivepence a pound for picking them: plenty of familites can earn six or seven pounds a day picking strawberries if the season is good. They're already on the dole and they're earning that amount of money. You see, it's different times.

I got it into my head to work for a horse breaker in March, in Cambridgeshire, by the name of William Lord Smith, but he wasn't a lord: it was his Christian name. We would be breaking horses – oh, eighteen or twenty – and at that time they used to charge four pounds to break your horse in and give you a load of corn and hay and straw as well.

Well that became a sort of dealing man's stable and I kept with old Smith until the beginning of the '14 War. And William Lord Smith had two hackney stallions that belonged to Sir Walter Gilby, who was a well-known hackney man in Norfolk and Suffolk country, and Mr Truman was a prominent veterinary surgeon of March, and these horses was handed over to old Smith for me to look after in my spare time – if I had any spare time because I was in the stable at six in the morning, home for breakfast at eight, and putting up horses at eight o'clock at night – but all for about fourteen shilling a week.

But there was a lovely family. One of the girls used to help in the house, and the other was a teacher, and old Mr and Mrs Smith was two lovely old people to me.

I couldn't afford to carry on with my lodgings – the landlady was charging me too much – and I said I'd be more at home in the harness house. Well the harness house had a stove and a gas ring, and I said I could make myself comfortable there: it was the life I'd been used to living. I said I'm not lost! I can manage myself. And I can save a few bob and have my clothes made at the tailor's, a pair of breeches in which I was trying to be a smart horsy boy, you know.

And the Italians and the Germans was coming over and buying the best horses in the country, even twelve months before the war started; and there was a lot of good hackney horses and blood horses bred in Norfolk and Cambridgeshire and they was sent to us. As fast as we could break them in buyers used to come and old Smith used to sell them. And then eventually the foreigners got stopped and the British army was looking for horses and every horse of any use was being commandeered. And plenty of horses were sent to be ridden, not driven, and old Smith used to break them. And I helped with that quite a lot. Until it come that the men were out of March and the streets was clear: they'd all volunteered. And I was the only sort of young fellow that was riding horses every day through the streets of March and out to Wimblington, and I seemed a lone ranger again. And the women used to look at me as someone that was shirking and one or two of them throwed a white feather at me, and I said: 'Get out of this!'

Old Smith said: 'Oh don't! What can we do? We've got no one else to work for us! Stop with me, Gordon. You can have the business if you want to!'

I could have got exempt from the army. He would have got me exempt because I was doing work of national importance. But no, I wouldn't. I said I wanted to go.

I wanted to go to the Veterinary Corps. I said: 'Do you think Mr Truman would give me a reference?'

He said: 'I'll give you a reference and so will Mr Truman.'

And they give me reference as a very good horseman, and I enlisted in the Veterinary Corps.

6

The Soldier

I JOINED the army in February 1915, and I was sent to Woolwich Common, to the 9th Lancer barracks where they received the Veterinary Corps people; and they put me in a riding ring on a wooden horse, and then on an old army horse, and then they sent me to a remount depot to ride green, useless, bronco-type horses: mustangs that were coming from Canada or America with a 'U' branded on – we used to call them 'Useless'. And they gave me three shillings a day when I passed my veterinary test at the Woolwich Depot.

I had to do bandaging of horses and giving them their points: nose, nostrils, ears, eyes, cuffs of neck, point of shoulder, the withers, the fetlock, the knee, the joint, the cannon bone, the splint bone and so on. And they said: 'Well this must be good – we'll pass him out First Class Veterinary Dresser.' And they give me fourpence a day for my rough riding spur. I wore it on my arm. I was very proud of this.

And they didn't keep me in Woolwich long.

They sent me to Salisbury Plain, to Bulford Camp, Larkhill. There were hundreds of horses there.

And they was vaccinating these boys, and I'd never been vaccinated in my life, and our people had always been against vaccination. And they tried hard to vaccinate me. Some of them tried to hold me down. But I wouldn't have it. And I know of no other man in the British Army that never was vaccinated. I had no mark on me. I wouldn't have it. They said: 'You'll get this disease and you'll get that disease!' and I said: 'I'll have it – I'll have all those diseases – but I will not have *that*! I will not be poisoned.'

Because we feared it. We feared it, as a Gypsy people. We feared anything like that, you see. My people didn't believe in it.

The Soldier

And one morning I was called up, and a few of us was put in a boat at Southampton, with a lot more, and we landed at Boulogne; and a few of us was sorted out, and we went to a veterinary hospital about three kilometres from Boulogne in some chalk pits. And there was a lot of sick horses there: shell-shock, ringworm, mange; and they put me on clipping.

Horses get shell-shock – off their corn – nervous – gradually wasted away. People, they only thought of soldiers in the war; I thought of horses as well, as they became a man's pal.[23]

And the better quality the horse the more susceptible it was to shell-shock. Well there was all these sick horses, lame horses, sick horses, some being condemned and going to the slaughter-house for the French Army. I believe they used to give nine francs each for a horse for human consumption for the French Army because we were allies at that time you see.

And in that camp there was Major Burrows, heavyweight champion of the Army and Navy, a fighting man. Very big man. He was a sportsman. And there was several sportsmen with him. There was Peter Langham, a wrestler from Burnley, Atkinson from Blackburn, and there was a trotting man called John Jones from Cardiff; he was my pal, he was a bit of a fighting man, and they wanted any sportsman, anyone who could box or wrestle. Peter Langham sent to his constituency Member of Parliament at that time (he was educated) and he got a wrestling mat, got boxing gloves, and John Jones, the trotting boy from Cardiff, he wrote to his Member of Parliament at Cardiff and they sent us boxing gloves and jock straps. And they picked out the best sportsmen.

Anyhow, I was picked out, at about ten stone four, and I could fight a bit, and I would wrestle because Peter Langham was my pal – he taught me how to wrestle in a little way on the mats. And I represented the Veterinary Hospital at Boulogne and I won the contest: I went about fifteen rounds, and I collected about fifty francs.

And eventually I was sent up to Number 10 Mobile Section, the First Cavalry Division. There were twenty-eight men and an officer, and a sergeant and a corporal. And of course this was going now into the beginning of 1916, and the Cavalry Division moved back again to Albert and I remember the sixteenth of July as well well as you're sitting there, when the cavalry charge happened.

And that cathedral at Albert – I don't know whether you've ever seen a postcard of it – but when they shelled it – there's a big angel on the top of Albert Cathedral – and somehow she was hit in the feet and she tipped over.

And she was looking down on the cemetery yard and when you looked up – especially a boy like me that was away from home, I never met any Gypsy boys, nobody belonging to me, I felt a lonely man – and when I looked up I used to think of my mother, when she used to say: 'Close your eyes my children. Let's bless the Lord for our daily bread today, the bread that's sent us.' And then my mind used to fly back to my mother.

And some of the boys pulled the coffins out of the big vaults – there's some marvellous vaults – they pulled some of the coffins, stone coffins and leaden ones, out of these vaults and they made dugouts of the vaults, had fires down 'em.

And the cavalry charge come just past the cathedral at the beginning of Carnoy Valley, and it was that very time when the Cavalry Division was a failure.

The valley was all long poppy fields and long alfalfa-type grass, and in it was nothing but hundreds of miles of barbed wire. And the horses was charged in that Carnoy Valley and they was all fastened up in wire on top of each other!

And it was our job to fetch out the wounded horses, my job to fetch the sick horses back: one that could walk a yard or two. And there was all chalk trenches there, and we'd prop up the poor wounded horse, and I'd shoot it, and we'd drop it in the trench. And that was our job: putting the horses out of their misery. Saddles and bridles on them as well, there was no time for anything.

And sometimes I remember the poor peasants coming

back through to Albert in bullock carts, the wounded, wounded children, and passing by Albert Cathedral; and on the chalky roads wounded Germans leaning on Englishmen's shoulders walking back. That was war.

We was under fire. And we had to move back with the horses, and we was sent out on our own to wherever there was horses running wild and we had to try and catch them. And there was several, I can tell you, and you couldn't get near them; you could see them in the distance. But eventually they all got caught and they was led back. The good ones that is.

And the cavalry charge was a failure.

I don't know whether it's been exposed by the war lords of that time, but it was a failure. Because after that the cavalry was dismounted. One man was left with four horses, to attend to them, and the other three was put in the line.

And they advanced through Carnoy Valley and up to Thrones Wood. I remember the Black Watch was there.

And I was riding a black horse, and I was sent on a dispatch to get in touch with somebody, I believe it was Major-General Meakins. And I was supposed to go to some headquarters, a dugout or something, and when we were coming back a shell burst beside my horse and we both fell in a shell-hole and my horse broke his leg. And I shot him, because I carried a revolver at the time. I shot my own horse, and I came walking back.

That was the first time tanks was in action. And there was three, very close to Albert Cathedral, three out of action – they'd been burnt out – and I slept in those tanks.

We slept anywhere we could get of course – bivouacs, or anything like that.

And there were some very funny characters about.

It was the time when the first Americans was coming over, American soldiers, and they seemed to be disbanded. Some of them got astray. And I remember we was in a dugout in Albert churchyard and we was having bully beef and biscuits, and we was smoked out with this fire of bits of sticks, this biscuit tin with a fire in it. And this American soldier with his marvellous clothes on, he come down the steps and he seemed to have the wind up. He was frightened, in my opinion. I think he was on the run. We thought so. And we give him a drink of the tea we had made, and we kept questioning this broad Southern American – the clothes was better than the man.

'Well,' I said to him. 'What do you think of the war now?'

'Well I guess we'll finish the God-damned war in six God-damned weeks,' he said.

But he was very loath to leave us the next morning, but our own officer, Lieut. Plunkett, he come down and give us some orders to go somewhere, and he found this American soldier and sent him off.

Now, I was sent by myself back to the Béthune front, to our sergeant-major, because he took the part of a veterinary man as well and I was to assist him, and we was attached to an artillery battalion. And that was very bad for us, because whenever we took the horses to water, in a canvas water trough, we got shelled and a lot of horses was wounded. And I was there six or seven weeks and they found why these horse were getting shelled at drinking time and they found out that it was a female spy that was close by. And I remember that she was brought out and shot, almost straight away. She was found in a farm, and she had some sort of contraption that she used to give signals when these horses were at the water and there was a lot of horses wounded.

And of course Béthune at that time was a sort of neutral zone because we didn't particular shell Lille that was opposite because there was a lot of French people over there and Germans too; and there was a lot of Germans left in Béthune. And it was a sort of steady carrying on, but it was never shelled much, Béthune, so it was partly inhabited, and we could go in there, and do a bit of shopping when we had time. And I had a French butcher that used to come and ask me if we had a wounded horse that wouldn't go down the

line to hospital, and he would buy it for ten francs or whatever, and I would probably keep the money, or some officer
would, you know. And that was life.

And now, you see, I went back to my Mobile Section – my
Number Ten Mobile Section again after a few weeks. And it
got the winter of 1916, and it was a very bad winter: very
severe frost, snow. I remember they bombed the bakehouse
at Boulogne and that was the only source of bread at that
time for the British Expeditionary Force and for weeks we
never had any bread. We were living on biscuits, and plenty
of people went down incinerators and found tins of pork and
beans that was blown, and a lot of soldiers was taken ill with
dysentery and so on. And that's all we lived on: biscuits and
bully and whatever we could get.

When horses didn't respond to treatment we put them in
wagons, eight in a truck, and sent them down the line to the
nearest veterinary hospital, and we went with them. It took
three or four days on that journey and then we would make
our way back as best we could.

We loaded hundreds of horses at a place called St Omar,
and they would go to any veterinary hospital that the railway line would take us to. It could be Boulogne, Abbeville,
Rouen or Le Havre. And anything going down the line had
to be shunted on a siding for ammunition trains and sup-
plies coming up to the front, and sometimes we would be
standing in sidings all night or a whole day before we could
move on. We would draw our rations from the Railway
Transport Officer, hay and oats, but we dare not open the
doors of the trucks to feed the animals as it was odds-on they
had gnawed their leaders, which were rawhide leather, and
eaten them. Of course, then they were loose, and only too
keen to get out if the door was opened.

Our rations were, even so far in the war, raisins and cur-
rants, flour, butter, bully beef, tea, and sometimes as much
meat as one of us could carry. Then we would have one truck
for ourselves and the rations. I would get a bucket to make a
fire in, and put holes in it, and with some coal from the
engine driver we had a fire, and lived on roast meat, or meat

fried in a dixie lid. I would make a cake with flour and raisins, and bake it on a bit of tin on the fire.

We were like sweeps after those trips – and all of us lousy too – but when we delivered our horses we usually got a new lot of clothes if we told the officer we were lousy. Of course the boys in the veterinary hospitals had good huts or tents and shower baths, and none had ever thought soldiers were lousy at the front.

Many times on getting back we found our section had moved further on. Wherever we were needed we would make our horse hospital, anywhere sheltered, or any old farmyard for them, and our own saddle horses, but most of the time we would be out in the open and we would make our bivouacs to sleep in. I could usually make myself comfortable. I would make a tent if I could find a few rods, and with two or three saddle blankets I would be alright with some hay to lie on.

Once we was in bivouacs, near the sick lines and horses tied on, and our captain was a little man called Captain J. J. Plunkett. He was an Irishman.

Now there were several people in our section, educated boys, that knew something of politics at that time – if you remember – there was some connection, if I'm right, with the uprising in Ireland at the beginning of the war with the Plunketts and Roger Casement. And these boys pointed this out to me. And he was a very strict little officer, very good horseman, very dandy little fellow, but very strict. And this rough night we were in bivouacs as well as we could, and it was frost and snow, and our horses was staked out, pegged out in lines with mud up to their hocks and knees. I never was a drinker but I did have a rum issue, when it come up.

And this particular night the rations hadn't come up at the right time, and my officer, Captain Plunkett, he was sleeping in the G.S. wagon, under the sheets. He was quite comfortable. Some of us was on guard, and it was all sorts of weather, and eventually the rations did come up after a long time in the middle of the night. And this rum issue come.

And there was several people wanted it, because we was all

shivering. And they said: 'Who will go and ask Captain Plunkett, can we have the rum issue?'

And I went to him – they picked me out to go and ask him – and he said: 'Certainly not! Don't bother me!'

I came back to the boys and told them that, and they told me to go back again, and I did, and then I said: 'The boys demand it! They're very cold. They want this rum issue! Can the sergeant dish it out?'

He said: 'No. Don't bother me no more!'

And the next morning they brought me on a charge and the charge was 'Insubordinate Language to a Superior Officer'. And they give me fourteen days C.B.

What the C.B. was made out to be I couldn't understand because we was practically in the front line and I couldn't see what they could put me to worse than that, but one particular man said: 'I wouldn't stand for it, Gordon! I should refuse to take this punishment and claim to take a court martial.'

And I thought, with my ignorance at the time: well I may get justice if I can plead my case for myself on behalf of the few men what was left in this section, and anyhow Leary said: 'Alright – we'll have a court martial for you.'

Eventually I was marched down to headquarters in a farmhouse, where all these red-ribboned officers was across on a table, and I was pulled between two guards and I pleaded Not Guilty. And tried to explain myself. And they marched me out – back to my section again under guard – and there was a general parade of my section and they had sentenced me to four months' First Field Punishment, and I had to be sent down the line to do it.

The mounted red-caps came and collected me and took me some miles behind the lines to their headquarters, which was another farm. And of course I was a good horseman and I cleaned the horses and saddlery, and I lived in their mess with them, and they knew I wasn't going to break out or anything – where was there to break? It was a good life anyway, and they all behaved well to me and they tried to keep me as long as they could.

It's funny, I really enjoyed three weeks or a month with them, and they didn't want to send me down: I was such a good fellow to keep the tackle clean. And I worked and worked and I thought: this is good! But eventually they said: 'You'll have to go, son.'

They took me further down the line to some more mounted red-caps and they put me on a goods train and sent me down to Harfleur Camp and what a horrible time!

It was in November and I had to come out in February, and the weather was terrible. And as I marched through this barbed wire compound and was handed over to a sergeant Military Police, and I had the photograph, I remember, of my mother and my two sisters and they searched me and they saw the girls and he was, you know, vulgar, and I snatched this photograph out of this policeman's hands and he was going to hit me and I said: 'If ever I find you – I'm a better man than you – as big as you are – if ever I find you ...' And of course I was in bad books from then on. But he said hard words about my sister's photograph, beautiful girl, you know, all sorts of vulgar talk – and I couldn't swallow that.

Anyhow, in that particular compound there was a barbed wire fence the way round and next to the barbed wire compound was a German prisoners' camp. They were getting food parcels wrapped up in calico. We were sleeping in bell tents that had been riddled with bullets – eighteen to a tent. And we was up in the morning at six for parade, knife, fork and spoon inspection, all cleaned with sand; if any speck of dirt which we'd been frying in a dixie or mess tin, a bit of black on it, they'd say: 'You see that speck of dirt? You'll get ptomaine poisoning! Go back to that sand heap.' And when you come back you were out of the queue and there was only half a dixie of black coffee and some broken biscuits and a bit of cheese and part of a loaf of bread to last you for the day.

And we was marched out at eight o'clock on fatigue and we was digging deep trenches in the sand and chalk, ten and fifteen feet deep. One was at the bottom, throwing it up to a stage halfway up, and another was shovelling it on top and by the time it got to the top it finished up on the one that was on the bottom. And then when we'd dug this trench we was told to fill it in again.

And then there was a big hospital opposite, and they was carrying dead out of it, and we was sent digging communal graves. And perhaps we'd get a job all round the camps on sewage-farms. But we used to like those jobs because we got an extra dixie of tea and a few short ends of cigarettes and things like that.

March back to the camp at dinner-time, half an hour break for dinner – more bully beef, or stew, most of it water – use your bit of bread that you'd saved, away at one o'clock back to work, back home at half past four, line-up, knife, fork and spoon inspection, and a drop more black coffee and a bit of cheese, line up at six o'clock, on parade, number off, make a mistake in numbers, about turn, quick march, gallop up this, double march that. And then we was backed up to a row of fencing and we was tied up by hands and feet back-to-back crucifix fashion and that was from six to eight every night.

On Thursdays it'd be bath night. We were to strip this side of the barbed wire fence, walk through, and get in this cold water. Little bar of soap each one.

That was the First Field Punishment, and I stuck it, and, understand me, I'm still a Gypsy at the time. There was no other Gypsy boy in that camp. Nobody to talk to. Black men, Canadians, Australians, all nationality of soldiers in that camp, something like one thousand one hundred.

And then in your tents and silence after eight and not a word. If there was talking, plenty of men was kicked to death for it. While you was tied up, officer would come with the sergeant-major behind: 'Get his hair cut – pluck a piece out!' Man would come round with a machine and cut it all off. 'Leave a bit on the front, sergeant – leave a little bit on the front!' And away the machines used to go and cut the lot off.

We wasn't men – we was numbers.

And it used to dawn on me how one British subject can treat another. It was wonderful how one British subject would treat another. That is what killed my faith in the army.

Blighty

WELL now, I thought, when my time was up, I would be sent back to either a veterinary hospital or back to my mobile section. But no, I was sent to Rouen, to the camp.

Now understand: I had never had any soldiering training. I'd never stood to attention with a rifle. I was sent to Rouen and on a camp there – a training camp where they were putting people in training and sending reinforcements up to various regiments that had been weakened by casualties.

And I remember I went to see a fight. There was a boxing ring there and I remember a very prominent fighting boy that was a sergeant gym instructor there and he was a very good man in civilian life. At that time we used to call him Johnny Basham. And old Jim Driscoll, a lieutenant, gymnasium instructor over the Expeditionary Force in France, he was a lovely fellow: a man getting on in the autumn of life with lovely curly grey hair – beautiful little man. Well, I tried to get a job and I thought to myself I might get a fight there if I can get to Johnny Basham. And I got in contact with Johnny Basham.

'I've had several fights when I was in the Veterinary Corps at Boulogne and that like,' I said.

'Well,' he said. 'We're training some boys here – come along in the afternoon and you can have three or four rounds with somebody your weight or with me.'

'I'd rather have it with you.'

I had several rounds of sparring, what they call a 'G' fight. I could either fight or I could give an exhibition of boxing at the time. Because I was very active. And I give him a bout or two and a few rounds, and he said 'You'll do!' and he got me a fight.

And I got introduced to Jim Driscoll, shook hands with him in fact, and I did get a few fights in Rouen.

But I was without a regiment you see. My regimental badge of A.V.C. was taken off my epaulettes and my cuff: I was like a stripped soldier. But I was brought up and they give me a new rig-out of clothes and a pack and they put me in the Cheshire Regiment and they sent me direct up the line.

Now I'd never done any fighting.

They sent me direct up the line on the off-shoot sector of the Somme – it was Hell Fire Corner. For a few days I just carried water up to the front line in petrol tins, and there were mules and horses that had been killed, new saddles, ammunition: all laid down on the duck-boards, rotting.

And I eventually joined the Sixth Battalion of the Cheshire Regiment: they called them the Bantams. And they was a regiment was very badly cut up. There was only ninety left of the old regiment. And we relieved the Black Watch and they put me Number Two on a Lewis gun and we never liked relieving the Black Watch because they was a daredevil lot and when they was relieved they generally emptied a magazine of ammunition at the Germans over the top and at that particular parapet the German trenches was very close. In fact you could see the lights of a dugout at nighttime.

It was a very quiet front line for a time because, I don't know what they called 'em, but they said when they found out what regiment was opposite they was more like English people than Germans.

When we would come back after a spell in the front line, to the reserve line, for a rest as the army called it, though the duties was more numerous then than up the front, consisting of carrying petrol tins of water, rations, ammunition – sometimes a mile and a half walking on duck-boards or dodging shell-holes, or else levelling gun pits, or maybe a burying party.

And then the mail would be called out, and everyone expected one, but only a few got a letter or a parcel. And when things was quiet at night several of us would get together and ask those who had letters how was things in old Blighty.

Some had good news, many had bad news. Some had wife trouble.

This news would usually come from the parents of some poor boy: some boy that had a sincere girl friend, finished altogether for him. No news for him. And the sorrowful part of all this was: ninety per cent of the soldiers had photos of their loved ones in their wallets, and was always eager to show them to one another at any time we had to spare.

We relied on one of our pals when we went up the line to keep each other's addresses, in case we didn't come back, and he would write to his parents or wives or sweethearts if anything did happen, which was often.

And to make it worse the conditions we were in: mud, lice, filth and discipline. Many of us were not in a fit condition to endure it. At least that is what we thought. But then we told each other that thousands of others were the same. Talks like this was necessary to keep the morale up, for it couldn't last much longer we told each other and that was a speech that was needed and used to the end of the war. It couldn't last much longer.

And when the young sixteen- and seventeen-year-olds come to us towards 1917 and '18 two of us 'old soldiers' as we called ourselves would be in charge of one young recruit, to keep him up to standard, and it worked in most cases too.

But for me, these things has never left my memory, at no time in my life, for long. I think too that it was such a contrast to my life as a boy, and up to going in the army. The contrast was, I think, the freedom, and travels, and different jobs I had done – hard at times, I know, but freedom. The happiness I had been used to took effect on me.

I must say I was no angel as a boy, or as a young man either. I was full of experience of most things of life good and bad.

And I managed better than most of my pals did in the war. I could make a cake of broken biscuits in the lid of a dixie or on a bit of tin. If I could get at the cook, as I very often did, to get a bit of raw meat I could roast it on a spit, instead of having it in stew, and with a few potatoes I had that special meal which in my idea was connected with cooking in the life of a Gypsy. And so, do you know, the thoughts that went through my mind while that bit of meat was roasting helped me.

For I would like to bet that with all the millions of soldiers in France and Belgium, and England too, of all nationalities, the smallest number of one breed was the Gypsy or Romany. Because the population of Romanies then was like today: very small. For we still haven't got a country we can call our own, I been told so many times and my forefathers also, and I don't suppose there's a spare country anywhere now that can be given us.

But in that war I should have loved to have the company of any one Romany, or Traveller or the like, to confide in. When I met anyone dark like us Romanies I would sound them with a few Romany words: no response – no Traveller.

My best company was when I was near any Bengalis or Gurkhas. I could get on with them. I used to swop words with them – some of their words were like our words. The change was good for me.

And we saw plenty of action. In the Bantams we was at Ypres, Hell Fire Corner, Passchendaele and we saw a lot of battles.

Anyhow, one morning in the front line, we were standing to on the parapet and I had this machine-gun – the other boy was sleeping in the dugout in the trench – and there was a barrage come, almost levelled our trenches, and the Germans come across.

And whether it was a trench mortar or a shell I do not know, but it burst on the parapet and it was like – something like a blue flame and bells in my ears – and really, I don't remember any more. But they told me afterwards when I come round at the first field dressing station that a shell had burst, and buried me, and I had been dug out.

I was full of muck and dirt, and I had a wound under this knee here, and some shrapnel in this leg, and splinters of shrapnel in other places, but my shoulder – I thought all this side of me was broken because I couldn't use it at all. And, oh, I was all bandaged round me and I was very dirty and filthy, and lousy too.

I was *covered* in lice. That was the worst of it. I was a clean boy at home. Every soldier was lousy. They issued us with tins of black powder to put down the seams of our trousers and coats to kill the lice; and if we were out of the line we would pull our clothes off and put them in an old portable engine called a fumigator, and you waited for your clothes and when they came back the socks would fit up to your toes and your shirt would be reduced to a singlet and you would find the shells of these lice on your shirt. And we used to say that the Cheshire Regiment lice were the biggest in the British Army. Our regimental mark was a red diamond with a black diamond stitched in the middle of it, and we used to say: 'When you've seen one of our lice well fed there's a red diamond on the back of him!' And we'd say if we could get to another regiment we'd swap one of our big ones for two little ones: we didn't mind increasing them, but we didn't want them as big as we had them, you see.

Anyway they bandaged me up, and give me some coffee to drink, but I did feel bad. And they sent me down the line in a horse ambulance.

They put us on a train and I got to Rouen, right beside the docks and there was an American hospital there: all tents, yellow-lined, satin-lined tents, and beds in them.

And I laid in bed (they still didn't bother to let me have a shave or a wash) and then after one or two days these American doctors with a cigar in their mouth – I could swear like hell on this: 'Say, boy – what's wrong with you? What's wrong? What's under that bandage?'

I say: 'You take it off and you'll find out, but give me a ticket to Blighty and let me get on my boat.'

But anyway there was something about this arm, and it began to wither and get all peely. It had been in the bandage so long you see, with sweat and so on, and pain. So they had the American nurses with them as well but there was more courting than attending to the medical profession, and the boys. That's where I had one objection to the Americans, and they could come with their hats on and their spectacles and their cigars a yard long with ashes ready to fall off and drop in any poor boy's wound: 'Say boy – what's wrong with you? What's under that goddamned bandage?'

'There's some pain under there so be careful how you handle me,' I said. 'And I'd like a wash. I'd like for you to bring some water and let me wash my face, and let me have a shave if one of the boys will give me a hand.'

'You'll be alright.'

Well they had me out of this bed, and they had me with a lot of students and when they unbandaged my hand they kept putting it in certain different positions: it was like it had gone with my shoulder and it used to get locked. And I used to collapse.

It was something that hit me just like an electric shock – it was a bone that was broken in my shoulder.

'Now this is a funny case!' they would say. There was no X-ray at the time. 'Now this man – it doesn't hurt *this* way – and it doesn't hurt *that* way – but when you put it up *there* . . .' And down I'd go.

'For Christ's sake bandage me up and give me a ticket for Blighty!'

I thought to myself: they're pinning on tickets for Blighty for everybody, but never Gordon. They had me for experiment. They had me in that hospital with all that punishment for six or seven weeks.

But the best of it was I found out there was the Indian Veterinary Hospital on the racecourse near and I knew my brother Lewis was there as a sergeant. And I sent word with an orderly – I'd been running Crown and Anchor[24] when I was normal and I'd always have a few bob with me you know, in a leather belt. I give him some money to take this message to the Indian Veterinary Hospital to find Sergeant Boswell and a note to say your brother Gordon's in the American hospital, such and such a tent, and I didn't think the boy would go you know, and that very evening my brother Lewis came to my bed. And there was George Husband

from Peterborough, another dealing man at that time, he
was with Lewis but he was a private. And they'd both come
to see me. And I'd have done anything to see my brother,
you know, because he was my favourite brother. We were
stuck together like twins. Never one didn't do anything
without the other.

And him being a sergeant, he was able to come every
afternoon you see. And at that time we could sell a few Canadian boots. A lot of Canadian soldiers were coming into
hospital and they didn't want no boots. They was lace-up
ones and I used to get a pair or two and my brother Lewis
would put them under his coat and march them off and sell
them to the Frenchmen or something like that.

And he brought me anything he could find to eat, and I
didn't care how long I stopped in that hospital then.

But there come a time for me to get better and I wasn't
better. I'm sure those doctors and nurses in the American
hospital delayed my getting better many months longer
than I should have been if they have sent me to England
sooner. They wouldn't have passed out in England for vets,
yet they all had more stripes on them than a zebra.

I was still bandaged up and they put me on the hospital
boat and I remember getting mid-ocean in the Channel and
submarines was about and the boat stopped, oh, it seemed
ages in the middle of this ocean. It was very rough. And we
got to Southampton.

And when I got on this hospital train they come round
and said: 'Where do you live? Where do you want to go?'
And wherever you wanted to go they sent you in the
opposite direction. I said I want to get to Lincolnshire, to
Boston, Peterborough or Skegness. So they sent me to
Huddersfield.

And it was called Royd's Hall and it was a consumptive
hospital, had been in peace-time.

It was late in the spring of 1918 you see, and I got into
Huddersfield and they washed me, and brought us a bit of
breakfast – egg I think it was – and they brought us a whizz-
bang, postcard you know: 'I am admitted into such and such

a hospital, I'm going on alright.' I sent it straight home to my mother, who was then at Skegness.

But I felt badly, all over, and I had this big lump in my groin, and I told the sister and she brought the doctor and I had acute appendicitis and it had to be operated on straight away. I said: 'I am not fit – I'm not fit to have it!' He said: 'You'll have to be – you'll have to be operated on at once.'

I'll never forget it.

Colonel Marshall operated on me. The wound is longer than I've ever seen appendicitis operation mark because there's about twelve stitches, it must be eight inches long. And I was in a very bad state, low in condition; and they put me in a private ward by myself and told me I'd developed pneumonia and bronchitis and what with the coughing – I bursted the stitches and I didn't realize this for days you know. And I had another operation, and was restitched again, and I remember my mother was sent for because the address was on this particular card.

My mother and father was sent for from Skegness. And it must have been the second time this wound bursted and I was in a bad way but just sort of pulling through and I remember the door of the ward was open in the passage and I saw my mother. She wore a very big thick Scotch cloak with a big head hood. And she walked by that ward door and I recognized it.

It was Mummy you see! And eventually Mother and Father come walking through and I was so excited with seeing Mother and Father that they took my temperature, and my temperature went up and they had to take my mother and father away again.

My mother and father stayed in Huddersfield for some days, before I was in a fit state to be seen, and you know I was between life and death. And what done me – now this is a truthful story – when people was on the danger list they send the parson to you. And they sent a parson and his wife to me and he prayed. And the lady, it would be his wife, brought some big lillies and they put them on a little box beside my bed and I could smell them and them smelt something like a funeral to me.

They were white, with a lip on.[25] She brought these and put them in this vase beside my head and I looked at them and I could smell them and I thought: well this parson's come and I'm going to die.

Because I was still a boy, you know, still a child if you like, so far as words was concerned like my Mummy – Mummy and Daddy, that was it. I thought to myself: *parson* – those flowers – it smells like I'm going to die. That's why he's come. I wonder what Mummy will say. Truth. And I sort of bucked up – I said this must not happen for Mummy's sake. And eventually I pulled myself together.

And Mother was able to come, and Father sat beside me, you know.

They'd still not undone this bandage and it had been on for weeks. Because I was in such a state – it was just stuck there – I was a one-armed man. Very little pain you see, but I was just propped up in bed. And then, eventually when my appendix wound burst and started discharging they put a silver tube in and that was a bad thing and it left a hole as big as a walnut for weeks and months. And when I got a little better they said: 'Now we must look at your hand and arm' – and, oh, it was like a piece of white bone you know, no flesh on it at all. And a masseur, a lady masseur, she come twice a day and she masseured it and massaged it and I did feel some movement, could move my fingers, but it was always a useless arm for months and months and months. And then they sent me to Huddersfield Hospital and there was a marvellous lot of people.

The mill girls was very good.

Each girl used to pick two wards or one ward, according to what money they collected, and they would bring us perhaps two cigarettes each, and some matches, and perhaps an orange, and some would bring us sweets. I was then in a bath-chair, to be wheeled out, and some of the girls used to come perhaps every other day and take me out and wheel me in the town, take me home to tea, and push me out on a Sunday all day and take me back to hospital.

They was a wonderful lot of people, the Huddersfield people.

And about this parson and his wife: when I began to get better he come and see me in my bed, it was after the *Titanic* disaster, and he told me that both him and his wife was in the water and they was washed down in the mouth of one of the funnels and being as they was close together they managed to hold on to the lip of the funnel and with the lift of the boat they was shot out again and they was eventually saved.

And I was sent to Bradley Gate Hospital, not many miles away, and that was a place where the British Dye Works was, and King George come there during the war and they wanted a Guard of Honour, and a few of us was picked for the Guard of Honour in blue hospital clothes, and I did shake hands with King George. I'll never forget that.

Then I was sent back to the army, up to Seaton Carew, and I was Class B. I didn't do any particular parades, and I was a bit of a scheming sort of fellow – I could tell a lot of tales.

We had a rotten sergeant-major. We was on the front at Seaton Carew in a big house, and the boys was down on the beach in a dugout walking guard along the water's edge, but I managed to get some pass forms out of the sergeant-major's office and I wrote myself out a pass or two and signed myself Captain Jones of 'L' Company and one thing and another, and I had plenty of money at the time and I had officer's clothes made and I was dressed up as a regimental sergeant-major! And when I used to get to Newcastle I could come through them station gates and they never looked at me, and of course my brother Gilbert lived near and I used to go and stay with him and pull these clothes off and walk about in civilian clothes. And I used to get on the train to Seaton Carew and leave these clothes in a barber's shop in West Hartlepool.

But I got picked up for it with the red-caps, anyway. I was arrested.

And I was shoved in the guard room at the Town Hall, and we was in a cellar, and we used to play cards. And there was a big grid-iron over the pavement of the Town Hall and we could see people's feet going over there; and when one of the boys got his time expired and went out we agreed for him to break one of these bars out one night so that this window let down, and we could put some money through for these little boys that used to peep at us to go and get some fish and chips from across the road. So what money we had we used to send these boys for two pennyworth of fish and chips three times and all like that, and we used to squeeze it through this iron.

Some kids used to blow with our money and some didn't.

But the Armistice was signed when I was in that cellar, and of course there was eighteeen of us in those cellars and we broke out!

Yes, broke out of the Town Hall altogether, and there was pickets in the streets but we done as we liked.

I walked back again, but not until I'd spent my money.

And then of course I put my name down for discharge. Mother had a business of some kind and I gave all sorts of excuses. And I was sent to a holiday camp and discharged. And that was the end of my soldiering career.

But I was really a bad soldier from the time of being put in the infantry.

Because I lost my pal – my horse. It was the only friend I had in the army, was the horse. And those sick horses I looked after, they seemed like I was looking after my own children. I was sorry for them. I was sorry for those horses.

And you would see a very good quality horse, and I used to cry that they came in the army to be staked out in the mud.

A horse like that was claimed as an 'officer's charger' and it was probably riddled with shrapnel, and we was putting tapes in his skin to get the discharge away, his coat would be torn up the wrong way, and he'd be shell-shocked in the line.

But another type of horse that wasn't so well-bred – he could stand it somehow. It was funny. Now I studied all this and people say: 'Oh the soldiers – the soldiers!' But I've always thought as well: what about the horses? Remember that we are a lover of horses – they've been our friends. Beautiful horses probably belong with a carriage and pair with the gentry – a blood horse, a good hackney horse – quality – where the veins would stand out when it was warm. Beautiful quality feet and legs. That horse couldn't stand the punishment of that gun horse, you know. There was a vast difference.

There was all qualities of horses, and there was all characters, all different temperaments. Some rotten, some born rotten, some born more good and *they* was the horses that used to suffer.

And they was just as downhearted as men were at times was horses.

I always thought that the horse had thinking periods. When he was left alone he used to think, and he used to fret and no doubt about it, horses would remember their original life, and where they'd come from. And then to come into battle.

And it was just like me.

I had come from a free life. And then come under this military discipline. And they treated you not as a child and not as a man. You were a *number*. You were just a number because the soldier was bought for one shilling: the Queen's shilling. But the horse would cost seventy guineas so the horse was more valuable than the man. That's how I looked on this life, and when I was put in the infantry I lost all interest in soldiering. I lost my pal – my horse.

But then again, I think the army was the beginning of me. Because I'd think: if I get free I'll never grumble again – no matter how my life takes me! And I tried to fight against this militarism, and overcome it.

And I may as well tell you that from the day of my dis-

charge I've had many a fight, and I've not won them all, but
've tried to defend myself in persecution. I've lived through
t, and I've got through it – and I've conquered something! I
have conquered it to such an extent that I'm accepted by
you, and I am satisfied that I have achieved something in
my life and I am at peace with myself.

Only I do sometimes think, and my thoughts go back to
my remaining class of people who are *still* being persecuted –
the people on the roads today – and they haven't got that
about them to defend themselves with as I had: the education that my father and mother blessed me with by sending me to school.

It's helped me.

I've got those people to thank, my mother and father.
Children, you *must* go to school for a week or a fortnight!'
Much as we was persecuted at that time. Because we didn't
like it! We was *forced* to go, and I thank my mother and
father ten thousand times for what they've done for me, and
many of my brothers and sisters who can read and write.

I knew very little when I left school. Because I'm more or
less a self-educated man. Through trying to be in business,
do some booking, carry a pocket-book, pencil and paper,
write a letter – I think it's beautiful. I've achieved something. Yet I can't do it properly, a hundred per cent. But it's
brought me a long way up for people of your education, and
other people's education, to listen to me. And I'm satisfied if
they call me an odd character. It'll do me.

Because I'm always looking for odd characters myself.

~ 8 ~

Up North

WELL, when I was discharged I was Grade B3 or something of the kind like that, and this particular doctor said: 'According to your record I can't give you a good character.'

I said: 'You can please yourself – if you throw me a suit of civvies over that table or let me go home I'll very soon find a suit, I don't want no character from the British Army!'

But anyhow I did get discharged with my papers V.G. – Very Good. And when they examined me they said I had valvular disease of the heart at that time. Well, I've lived a long time with it – I don't think he was a very good doctor. And I got a pension of twenty-six shillings a week for sixteen weeks, and then they brought me up to Lincoln to be re-examined, and I queued up and it come dinner-time and they gave me eighteen pence for my dinner and I had to come back after dinner and queue up again, and I didn't manage it that day and had to come back the next and I thought I'll go. I wouldn't wait. And they reduced my pension to sixteen shillings a week, and after sixteen weeks they told me my ailment was not aggravated by war service and so I finished with the pension and got my gratuity money – thirty-six pounds.

And I bought two old ponies. I bought one for fifty shillings and the other one for thirty-five shillings, an old bent-back pony, and they was both white ones.

And then I got married and I went away on my honeymoon for four days to the Victoria Hotel and when I got back my best pony had died!

My mother had a house and shop at Skegness then, a fruit shop and they called it Covent Garden Fruit Shop. And my sister had a stall on the front in the season selling ice-cream and fruit. And we still had our wagons down on Cavendish Road.

But of course I got the rambles on me again, and I had a few bits of deals with scrap, and got a bob or two and got a better horse, and had a few deals with the baker and butcher and swaps and changes and buying old harness and repairing it. I was good at saddlery. I was putting old sets of harness in markets, and buying chickens and selling them to the shops, and going as far as a wood mill and getting a load of sawdust and selling it to the shops – at that time fruit shops, public houses and butchers' shops had sawdust on the floor.

My oldest boy was born in January 1921, and I was getting on alright. Getting a few pounds together in the horse trade, and going to sales at that time. There was plenty. I was buying scrap, and carving it up and putting it on rail, and, with other boys, we were making a trade between us, and getting a few quid, and what with a bit of dealing in lead it wasn't long before I had a few pounds. And I gave seventy pounds for a wagon.

I wanted to get out of Skegness.

It was a cul-de-sac. If you went one way you went into the sea and you had to come back again before you got anywhere inland, and if you went the other way you came into the sea too. It was all wrong to me.

Skegness at that particular time – why old John Moody was mayor of Skegness. He used to drive a landau with an old horse over on its knees, and old John had a suit of clothes on that his grandfather had had and it was going green. He was mayor of Skegness for twenty-eight years, I believe.

This old cob horse over at the knees that used to pull the landau – it was about twelve-two in front and fifteen-one behind, and I once said to him: 'That's Polly Perkins, Mr Moody, your horse! It's mother was a worn-out cab horse in London!'

'You mind your own business!' he used to say. 'It does the job better than some of the crooked things you're selling!'

No, Skegness wasn't my sort of country at all, and I bought a little Gypsy wagon for seventy pounds.

I got some harness together, and bought a decent old

horse for the shafts, and a couple of old ponies I had and I said: 'Yorkshire me! Up North! I'll get out of this and get to somewhere there's some population.'

And I bought this horse: it was a broken-winded horse, it was a good type of horse to rob a man with at that time. It was a good-*looking* horse. And I brought him up from the field – he'd filled his belly – and I got five mile on the road and we was going up a bit of a hill and he stopped, this horse, and a few drops of blood come from his nose and he started shivering and he laid down in the road and rolled over and he died!

Only five mile away from home.

I thought: this is luck. And I sent for a knacker and he give me twelve bob for the horse. I'll never forget that. Couldn't get another penny from him. He give me twelve bob for my horse and I had nothing to put in the shafts big enough; and I said – I thought to meself – well I'll have to pull off the road, and I hadn't got enough money to buy another horse without selling these two ponies and I thought what should I do? I've never borrowed a penny off my father in my life and I never intended to. But anyway, I went back to Skegness on a bicycle, told my father what happened, and he lent me *his* horse; and I rode it back to pull my wagon back to Skegness. And I had to have a few more weeks' work and trade – and still itching to get out of it – and I sold my two ponies and bought an old horse and away I went up into Yorkshire. And I got to Bingley.

To get back on the road, it was beautiful.

It was everything I wanted.

I still intended to go whether the horse lived or died or whatever. I couldn't help it. I didn't, I don't, like seasides today. I wanted to get away from it.

There was something in me bones that – I was a free man again!

Of course I was getting broke, and having these terrible losses – your horse you know – and horses wasn't cheap, a decent horse at that time. About thirty-six pounds I give for this horse. If it had been a sound horse it would have been worth seventy pounds: but there was that chance in my mind of selling it to somebody for seventy pounds. I should have hung about and I should have looked for somebody else to have bought that horse – because we was there to be shot at and it was the best man won.

I had no mercy.

Because when people come home from the war, it was the hardest thing in the world for a discharged soldier to get a living. People had already got what there was to be got and there was nothing for a soldier boy to come home to. And I felt this way – I was like a lion, seeking whom I may devour! I had no mercy – when I found a mug I made a sergeant of him!

It was me that mattered. Because they'd had me for nothing.

And I moved from Bingley to Bradford, and there was a bit of trade there. And then I went to Otley in Yorkshire and there was a pit pony buyer there who used to come and stay with me at Skegness with Mother and Father, from Great Preston; and I went with him and got so I could find a few pit ponies out of the pit; and he was putting better ones down, and I was buying a lot of old ponies off him and there was a fair connection with flat-cart boys with a cheap old pony. I could get these old pit ponies cheap and sell them for pulling hawkers' carts. And I went to plenty of fairs, of course, round Leeds way – Whitby Fair, Halifax Fair, Huddersfield Fair – why, there was fairs all round at that time.

I went from one to the other. Taking something, swopping on the way, buying and selling, and of course it was all horses. Old Jack Wilks used to have a lot of horses from Ireland every week. They used to send him as many as seventy horses and ponies a week and if he had anything left on his hands another week he would call them his 'unlucky horses' and he would say: 'Go and have a look in Number 7 Stable or Number 17 Stable and there's two or three in there. How much will you give for them?' So I used to hit him below the belt – he didn't want them. He called them his 'unlucky horses'. He died thousands of pounds in debt. They all said that Jack Wilks if he'd made five shillings a head profit on his horses in his lifetime he'd have finished a millionaire. But he died in debt.

Some of those army sales old Jack Wilks would go to York and if he was in the mood he wouldn't let any man have a horse. He'd buy the lot. And then he'd turn round and make two pounds profit on anything. Perhaps he'd take two pounds profit on a horse that was worth thirty pounds and he'd expect to get two pounds profit on something that cost him ten. An uneducated old man. He had some sons that were working for him but when he died I believe his boys didn't do any good. They emptied the stables, there was no further horses come. They turned the yard into a car auction and that business disappeared.

Jack Wilks wasn't a Gypsy. He was a Travelling man, part Irish I think. He had two wives in his life and I believe he had an awful lot of children, and his son-in-law used to send him these horses from Ireland every week.

Of course, if I sold an old horse to do a job for you I would charge you as much as possible for it. Character was nothing. I give 'em all good characters. They was the best in the world! That was salesmanship. That was horsemanship too. It was no good saying there was two characters about a horse – because I dealt for seven years in horses and I never had a good one apart from the one I drove. There wasn't many I couldn't drive.

There was good horses about but they was beyond my range of buying them. If you made a mistake in buying a horse from me the first loss was the best, and I'd come to buy it off you again and I'd say: 'Well I know that horse!' and you would have to sell it to me and it was certain profit for me when I took that horse off you again. I would then look for a villain to buy it off me, but if I couldn't find a villain, if I found anyone who was straight enough, if he had the money I should charge him plenty for it. *All* my horses was good ones.

I moved about in my wagon and I had regular stopping

places, and Yorkshire was more or less free. There was good places to stop.

And I got so I dealt in a different class of animal, and I got so I could sell a coalman an old horse, honest old slave, and let him have it on a week's trial and if it suited I'd get paid. Or a grocer wanted one, or an ice-cream man wanted one, let him have a trial with it, and if it suited him I found out it was an easier deal – contentment of mind on both sides.

When I was living in Leeds in the nineteen-twenties, I had my wagon at Meanwood, in the old White House Laundry, some stables and a field too I rented. I was buying lots of ponies from the collieries that were returned as bad workers, *convicts* I called them, and trade was good for a pony that would go in harness.

There were a lot of Italians living in the York Road area, which was slum property, and the Leylands too. Dozens of these fellows were ice-cream sellers, and all used a pony or horse for their work, and good customers too, but it was difficult to understand them as most of them hadn't been in England long. There were big families too, all ice-cream vendors, Antonio this, Antonio that.

I had a pony, his colour was blue roan. He had his winter coat on, so I clipped him all over, legs too. He looked smart with a good set of harness in my Liverpool gig I used for showing, so I drove to York Road among the Ities and one took a fancy to my pony. I sold it for fifteen pounds to him. It was broken-winded, a *widd*. The very next day I drove a black pony to the Ities. It was getting another Antonio interested, but he wouldn't buy it because it was a long-haired pony. He had seen his neighbour's pony, with short hair, and wouldn't have any other. He kept saying: 'Me want bluey pony with shorty hair. No hair blows in the ice-creamy.' So I said to myself: 'Antonio shall have a blue pony with shorty hair,' and I drove home and clipped the black pony out, and, of course, usually black ponies clip out a bluey grey colour, and I drove back to Antonio. I exchanged my blue pony with the shorty hair for his pony with the long hair, and I clipped his pony out on returning home.

A few days after this, my first Antonio drove to my stables with his broken-winded pony. He must have made lots of inquiries as to where I had my stables, because I made it a rule never to give my address to any of the Antonios. They weren't too polite if they got one of my cut price shorty-haired ponies, and this one was wild, with a knife in his hand, threatening me with it. I got the stable fork and he cooled off a bit. When I found out what his complaint was, he says: 'This pony is concertina, always blowing like concertina, no wind to pull cart, no-good pony for icy-creamy, good shorty hair, but no wind. Concertina. No good.'

I told him he must have fed him wrong and poisoned Concertina. 'No, no, he get good oatey oatey' (he meant oats). I must give him his money back he said, or another good pony with shorty hair. I told him I only had one more pony with shorty hair, and that was ordered for another Antonio, but he meant having a fresh pony, so I put his neighbour's pony in my trap and gave him a drive. I finished by swapping for the Concertina pony and I got some money too.

I had a few more complaints after that, but the funny thing was, at that time, they thought these shorty-haired ponies came from another country, and as I was the only one that clipped his ponies I had plenty of business with the shorty-haired cobs. But it only lasted until the hair started to grow to normal: I had to make myself scarce up the York Road for a time after that. Don't think, either, that these Antonios were angels. Oh no. They could give a kid a ha'penny cornet and set a bit of ice-cream on it no bigger than a walnut, and never a bit in the cornet. They hawked their cream all the winter dressed in a white shirt, but always two or three fishermen's woollen jerseys under it.

All these tricks of the trade have gone and forgotten a long time now, never to come again. The men that did these things, most of them are gone, and those that are alive today are old, and not in the trade. Most, I think, turned to the scrap trade or the motor trade. They had sons that knew things were changing, and the motor taking the place of the horse. I think in the car trade today, especially the used car, the tales of this wonderful car or lorry which the high pressure salesman are using today is similar to the horse trade tales, for I'm sure there are as many vehicles returned by dissatisfied customers today, and a lot more money involved too, as there were when the horse trade was plentiful in the nineteen-twenties.

And these men – these old horse dealing men was characters. And the old Travelling and Gypsy people.

There was old Jobie Lee, the old fighting man, he's long since dead. He fought with Pedlar Palmer and Joe Clarke and he won fifty pounds. And he had an adviser and this man told him not to waste his money but to put it in the bank, and he said: 'Have it as a current account and the manager will give you a cheque book.'

He did this, and he couldn't sign his name, so it was usual for a Gypsy man to sign it with a cross. And the adviser said: 'You can draw five pounds out when you like and how you like, and take care of your money and you won't waste it.'

So after a time Jobie kept drawing these five pounds out and five pounds out till he overstepped the mark with ten pounds. But the manager faced the cheque and he got in touch with this adviser and he said: 'Tell Jobie that he's overdrawn, and he can't have no more money.' So the adviser went to Jobie Lee and said: 'Now you're overdrawn ten pounds more than what we put in the bank, Jobie.' But Jobie said: 'You tell that bank manager he's a bloody liar – because I've got four more cheques left in me book!'

And then there was old Hutty, old Bill Townsend's wife, Hutty Townsend. During the '14 War somebody bought a newspaper, the *News of the World*, and there was a battleship on it, and she was holding the paper upside down, because she couldn't read, of course. And she called all her relations together and said: 'Oh my children, come and have a look at this terrible thing! It's a shipwreck!' But it wasn't – it was just that she held the paper upside down.

And she had heard that the boys were joining the army to go fighting. And she called about half a dozen soldiers to her once and she said: 'Look, my boys – what do you want to keep fighting and falling out for? Take this sixpenny piece and be good boys and get them awful clothes off your backs.'

And another Travelling boy from up North, he's dead now, they called him Rough House Baker. He was a well-known character up in Yorkshire. He was stopping at Ripon in his old wagon, and him and another two boys was out tatting for rags and they had a tin of goldfish – they was Japanese goldfish, and of course there was a lot of them in one of those tins, and they went out and they'd give these goldfish for rags and they got a lot of rags and they had a good day.

And they sold the rags and they all went on the beer, and they had enough money after one day's work to keep on the beer for two days. But there was half a tin of goldfish left, and when they sobered up after the second day Rough House said: 'We'll have to go out and get a living of some kind – we've got a few goldfish left. We've got a few left for swag!'

So one of them said: 'You're disappointed this time, Rough House! They're all dead! They're wasted!'

'No they're not!' said Rough House. 'We've got nothing for breakfast. I'm going to fry the buggers!'

So he put the goldfish in the pan and fried them for breakfast.

Then there was old Watson. He was a very old dealing man. He bought anything and everything. He used to take the worst horses of the fair – the villains, the hooks, the laymens – casualties he called them. Only he called them *cash*-casualties – not casualties. And anybody who had something left on their hands they'd say: 'Watson, take this and do the best you can!' And sometimes he'd pay for it and sometimes he wouldn't.

But after the '14 War I remember he was dealing in a lot of army horses – him and Billy Wilson, another old-timer that's gone, and they had two men working for them. One was called Sawdust and the other was called Cut Throat, two men that understood horses but never had a lot of money, of course; but they was hard-working men. And they had a lot of these *cast-casualties*: when the fair was over at Appleby they has seventeen horses between them and they hadn't got *one* that could pull the two wagons. They had to borrow two horses to pull the wagons across so you know the kind of characters of horses they dealt in!

But at that particular time there was a lot of dud one-pound notes being spread about in Leeds, and several of them come into my hands and several to other dealing men. They was a yellower note (this was the time of the red ten-shilling note) and when John Bradbury was signed on them, though they was a bit thicker than the ordinary notes, we got them by, actually.

But Watson had about forty of them, and he didn't notice it until he was counting his money and he saw the difference. So he said to Cut Throat and Sawdust: 'Take this money and divide it between you and go and buy something at the fair and bring what you can back.'

And they did so, and they went on dealing and they thought they'd got shut of these dud notes. But then it was getting near the end of the fair and they sold one or two horses, somebody come up and bought the horses, and they had the money for them and when they handed this money over to Watson he'd got all his dud notes back – they'd worked them back to him again!

There was Abraham Wilson, another well-known Travelling man. And he had a big family, many of them's living today. And it was a time after the '14 War when a few of the wealthier Travelling people was going over to motors at that time, and he bought one for his girls to go out hawking, and one of his boys was driving this when he learned to drive, and old Abraham was so excited with this Ford – he'd been out in it for the day – and when he come home some Travelling people was asking him how he liked his Ford and he said: 'I think it's the most wonderful thing in the world for a Travelling man. That boy's been on the run with it all day long and it's been running all day on a bucket of water!' You see he'd seen the boys put water in the radiator but he'd never seen them put petrol in the tank and he thought it ran on a bucket of water. He said: 'It's a waste of time having horses, feeding them and getting fields for them when you can put a bucket of water in a thing like that and run about all day. Cost you nothing! We've been fools to have horses for years. We ought to have had these years ago!'

That was old Abraham Wilson. He was very deaf, a lovely old fellow, a real old Romany Joe. They've got some of the family left at Skipton, a well-known, well-liked family.

Then there is a well-known character – his name is spread about the country – old Paddy Murphy from Preston. He was a good old horse dealer, liked a good horse or pony, but many years ago, when horses was the way of transport, he used to advertise a lot of old things in the papers, looking for mugs of course. He had an old grey mare with no teeth and very poor and so on, and he advertised it in the paper like this: 'For sale, must go to good home. Blossom, quiet and a good worker. First thirty pounds it's yours.'

A wire come: 'Please put Blossom on the train to Lancaster.'

He wires back: 'Please send cheque for thirty pounds for Blossom.'

So the cheque come and he waited a couple of days to get this cheque through the bank for his thirty pounds and the man wired again: 'Haven't received Blossom yet.'

'Delay in ordering truck – Blossom will be on rail on Thursday.'

On Thursday he wired: 'Blossom arrives at twelve o'clock at Lancaster.'

So he puts it on the train and two or three days later a letter comes to Paddy. It says:

Dear Mr Murphy,

I have received Blossom. It has no teeth, it can't eat properly. A dealer tells me I should boil potatoes for it. It's too weak to work – it's no earthly use to me at all.

If you don't come and fetch Blossom away I shall sell it to the Gypsies.

Paddy used to deal in hens as well, and anything he could deal in. He had an old stable and he bought some light-weight hens and he put them up in the loft and he told this boy that worked for him that was a bit light in the head that he had a customer for these hens and he said: 'Take this two shillings and go to the shop and buy me two shillingsworth of the biggest eggs you can find.' And then he said: 'Go up into the loft and spread these eggs about with a big of chaff – I've got an old man coming to buy these hens.'

So he met the old man in the public house and he said: 'I've got a beautiful sample of hens for you today so come and have a look.'

After they'd had a drop of beer Paddy took him to the stable and there were steps up to this loft, and he said: 'Go up there and have a look at the hens!'

So the client's up there a bit, and he comes down and Paddy said: 'Well what do you think, Tom?'

He said: 'They're all right, Paddy.'

Paddy said: 'They're laying as well.'

'Yes,' the man said, 'I see that. I want to buy your hens, Paddy, for one thing. I'm not going to give you *your* price for them though. I'm buying them for one thing.'

He said, 'What for?'

'Well,' he said. 'It's the first time in my life I've known a White Wyandotte who laid bloody duck eggs!'

My poor brother Eden, passed away a long time ago, I sold him an old stallion pony, a good sort, had come out of the pits round Wakefield, and he travelled about with his little wagon on his own, and he was making his way to Hull Fair, the eleventh of October.

And when he got just outside Hull where we used to stay he met a pal of his, just before the fair, and this pal had a little sucker, we called it: a yearling pony – and he said to my brother: 'Well take this to the fair and sell it for me.'

So he tied it to his old pony's neck and away he went to Hull Fair, and when the two of them stood together a young fellow come along and having a look at these two ponies which he thought were a mare and a foal.

And my brother said: 'Would you be interested in them, Sir?'

He said: 'No,' he said, 'but I should buy the mother. I don't want the foal – I've got no use for the foal – but I could try to buy the mother off you.'

'Well,' he said, 'she's a good sort of mare. And I should sell her quiet and a good worker. She's a very good animal.'

And he sold this fellow this stallion, and the poor boy thought it was the mother of this foal.

Of course the fellow never come back because the fair was over that day. It was a one-day fair, so it was ta-ta to the goods. And the amusing thing was – my brother was supposed to be a good-living man – he wasn't supposed to do anything wrong to anybody. He was a religious man. And I thought to myself: he's like a lot more; he didn't want to miss this customer!

Then, oh, Oiney Lee, one of the old North of England Travelling people. Well known as a fighting man: he always clipped his hair very short and he had scars all over his head when he was in fighting form; he used to take the felly of a wheel and hit himself with it, make his head bleed as though he had no pain in it, to make himself such a hard man.

But he used to tell the tallest stories any Gypsy man ever known and this is one of them:

He had an old dog that was a very, very good coursing dog. It was a bitch, and he got her coursing over a field but the old bitch was heavy in pup and it coursed this hare and it failed to catch her, and eventually it broke the confinement – and gave birth to six puppies! And of course Oiney left them lying there and he went back to his wagon. And later on in the day this old bitch comes back with a hare in its mouth, and the six puppies, each one had killed a leveret and had fetched these back. For the bitch had had six puppies and the hare had had six leverets, and each pup had killed a leveret.

One of his favourite lurchers died, and he had a pair of leggings made from the skin. One day he was out coursing with these on and, his present dogs not being as good as his

The tombstone, at Tetford, Lincs., of Tyso Boswell and Edward Heron slain by lightning in 1831. (The common Gypsy name of Heron has various spellings including Hern, Hearn and Herne.)

Below: Gordon's
mother, Athaliah,
in 1921.

Above: Gordon's fath
Trafalgar Boswell, *cir*
1930. His clothes wer
made in Spilsby from
material used in a sui
for the Prince of Wal

Coming over the Pennines with horses bought at Brough Hill Fair, 1913.

Oliver Lee, 1913.

Matthew Wood, 1914.

Jack Woods and family, Yarm Fair, 1928.

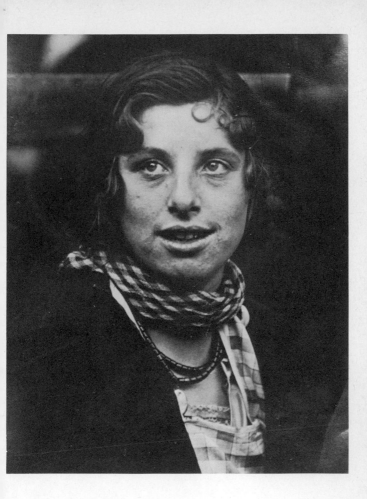

Tilley, daughter of Jack and Nation Woods.

Above: Smiths and Coopers, Epsom Downs.

Below: Nelson Lee and his wife, 1923.

Above left: Ithal Lee, 1938.

Above right: Nation Locke, daughter of Būi Boswell.

Below: Lily Macfarlane, daughter of Oliver Lee, 1939.

Eastern Counties Travellers in front of an ex-Army tent.

Above: Members of the Gyspy Lore Society in front of a rod tent, 1912.

Below: Detail from a decorated caravan.

Above: North Country Herons
on the road.

Below: Dennards and Beldams,
Epsom Downs, 1923.

'Black Amos' Herne and wife, 1916.

Jim Thorpe's brush wagon, 1910.

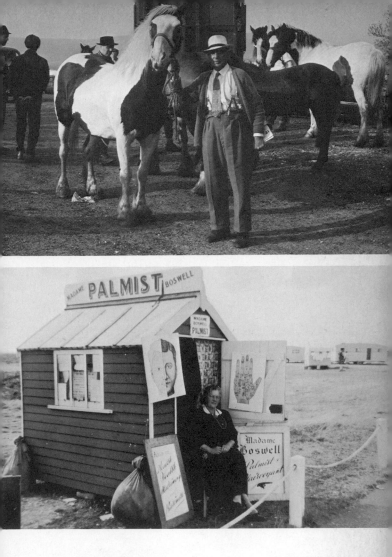

Above: Gordon Boswell at Appleby Fair.

Below: Gordon's wife, Mabel, at Rockley Sands, Dorset.

Above: Gordon Boswell, 1961.

Below: Gordon and Mabel Boswell with their trailer.

old dog, the hare was having the best of the race. But his leggings flew off his legs and held the hare long enough for the dogs to kill, leggings then returning to their rightful place on his legs again.

And he was an old man liked fishing for eels, all Travelling people like eels, and he was keen on looking in ponds and fishing for big old eels and he looked in this particular pond and found some big old tanks, and he said: 'I went and got my knife out and scraped one and they was all copper, and I weighed them in for scrap and made meself enough to buy a new wagon with. And of course when I got the wagon I thought it was a lucky place to stop and so I went fishing in this very pond and I caught the biggest eel I ever caught in my life! It took me all evening to pull it to the side, and it was far too big to eat, so I skinned it, and put the skin on the hedge to dry, and I didn't know what to do with the skin, but I thought to myself somebody can do with it, so I cut this eel skin in half and sold it to two farmers for two stack covers!'

Another pal of mine who's passed away, we called him Cheeky Simpson but he went for three names, Charlie Simpson, Cheeky Simpson, and Captain Simpson. And he lived around Bradford for many years and it was a time they was calling people up for the army during the last war and he had done a bit of *stir*[26] for some short periods for different things. And when they called him into the examination room and was taking his particulars the officer said: 'What's your occupation?'

Charlie said: 'I'm a professional burglar.'

'What?'

'I'm a professional burglar. I get my living by burglary.'

'Well,' said the officer, 'we can't have you in the army with a character like that you've given yourself.'

'Well I'm willing to go,' he said. 'If you'll put me in.'

But of course Charlie didn't want to go, and that's how he got his total discharge from the war. They didn't want professional burglars in the army.

Another old Gypsy character long since gone called Sammy – I won't tell you his other name. He was reckoned to be a wicked old man. But he and my father went on a train to go to a fair at Preston: Preston New Year's Fair, to buy horses and the kind. And he got up very early, and he woke up Father and they got on this station and the train wasn't due for another hour. And he was cursing and swearing about this train being late for him, and when the train did come in my father got in the carriage and he said: 'Come on, China, get in!'

'Oh no!' he said. 'I've waited for that – let that wait for me!'

'Well,' said my father, 'it won't wait for you.'

'Well,' he said, 'I'll have next time. But I won't lower myself to ride on *that* train. I've waited for it long enough.'

Why he was reckoned a very wicked man:

He had a horse in his wagon and when he got to a hill – it wasn't a very good worker this horse – this horse stopped on the hill and Sammy blocked the wheels and he couldn't get it to pull any further. The horse tried his best to move it but he couldn't.

So Sammy prayed, he prayed to the Lord to give this horse power to pull this wagon up the hill. And after he'd prayed he got hold of the horse's head and it *still* refused to pull.

So he said: 'Well I've tried the Lord – I'll try the Devil now!'

So he got on his hands and knees at the side of the road and he prayed to the Devil to give this horse power to pull his wagon up the top of the hill, and after he'd prayed to the Devil he got hold of the horse's head and said: 'Gee up!' and away went the horse and pulled the wagon to the top of the hill.

And when he got up to the top of the hill Sammy stopped the horse and patted it on the neck and he said: 'There you are! I prayed to the Devil and the horse has gone up the hill. I prayed to the Lord and He's supposed to be the good man and He wouldn't give my horse power.'

So he said: 'Lord – I'm just going to pull my clothes off and if you'll come down here I'm going to give you the best hiding you ever had in your life!'

This Sammy at Nottingham, he liked his drink, and my father was in his company at that particular time and old Charlie Boswell, and they were all three pals, but Sammy used to drink more than what the others did and he got a bit obstreperous in a public house and he got arrested.

And he didn't arrive at night and his people was worried about him and so my father and Charlie Boswell went to look for him in Nottingham.

And they said: 'Well he must be in some public house. When they turned out he might be locked in.'

But they was going down to the police station thinking he'd be in there, because he'd been in several times before.

At that time if the police got a drunken man they used to have a little two-wheeled stretcher-ambulance and strap them on, you know. And coming down this street was two policemen wheeling somebody on this stretcher-ambulance, and the policemen pulled them up and said: 'Who are you?'

Charlie Boswell said: 'This is my cousin on here.'

'Oh,' the policeman said. 'He's a nice cousin too!'

So Charlie reached over to Sammy and said: 'Your wife's upset about you.'

Sammy said: 'Tell her not to worry.'

And he said to my father: 'How do I look?'

So my father said: '*Kushti!*'[27]

And Sammy waved his hand and said to the policemen: 'Drive on, then!'

But he ended up very queer.

He used to stop at Sutton near the River Trent at Nottingham, Retford way, with the wagons. And he was seen to walk out of his tent or wagon one night and went for a walk down this lane, down the riverside. And he never returned.

They dragged the River Trent for many days for him but they never found him. And some people said that the Old Man, his Old Friend, had picked him up and took him to his destination. That's what some people said about him at that time he disappeared. He never was found, wasn't this

Sammy. Never was found. But finished up in the River Trent, I always thought.

Years ago there was supposed to be an old Travelling man, a very good horseman, and he bought a horse and it had fairly long teeth.

So he was *bishoping* these teeth as we call it: he had a hacksaw and he was shortening these teeth and trying to make it into a younger horse.

And a little Traveller boy, not very old, that lived with his mother, he come across and was watching this old man bishop this horse's mouth.

He said: 'What are you doing, Uncle?'

'Well, my boy – I'm trying to make this horse into a four-year-old horse.'

'Are you, Uncle?'

'Yes.'

'Well – my Mummy's old mare is very old and it's got very long teeth. Could you make it younger?'

'Yes, my son. I could.'

'How much would you charge me?'

'About half a quid.'

'I'll go to my Mummy and ask her.'

So he told his Mummy, and his Mummy gave him half a quid and he took the old horse across to the Travelling dealer man.

He said: 'There it is. I want you to make it into a younger horse.'

So when he'd finished his own the dealer said: 'How old do you want this mare, my son? Do you want it three-year-old or four-year-old?'

So the boy said: 'Oh Christ no! Make it seven or eight years will you, Uncle – else the old bugger will run away with my Mummy!'

There was a well-known man who lived in Shipley: they called him Lancs. I never knew his other name. He was a very good gambler and he used to drive a very good horse at that time, a hackney, and if it got steamed up it would have a bang at a cat, and they called this pony 'Peggy O'Neill'.

But he drove from Bradford to Leeds auction one Tuesday, and he got in with the lads, and his turn-out was valued at a hundred pounds. So Billy Wilson had another turn-out of a similar value, and Lancs from Shipley said, 'Well, I toss you up who takes the two!'

And they tossed up, and whether it was a double-headed penny or not I don't know, but Lancs lost his bet and he had to hand over Peggy O'Neill and his gig.

And Lancs went on the beer a bit that day, and he said: 'Well I'll finish the day off in style!'

So in those days there was a charabanc about, so he hired a charabanc, and he bought himself a cigar, and he sat in the back seat and had the charabanc drive him home to Shipley!

I once went to Appleby Fair with him and he said we was going in partners. He was always a toff, well dressed. And I met him at Shipley with my wagon, and I didn't tell him what money I had, but I had the horses and a few pounds and he looked like he had some, and when we got into Kirkby Stephen he went into a public house. He was rather a strong drinker – I didn't drink at all – and they carried him out of the public house unconscious.

They'd doped him, or something of the kind.

And they put him in my wagon and I was disgusted at having a drunken man asleep in my wagon, and when I got to Brough Hill he woke up. And he felt in his pockets and his money was gone. And the worst of it was – he accused me of robbing him.

Whether he was working one over me or not I don't know, but he accused me of robbing him which wasn't the truth.

I give Lancs the best hiding he ever had in his life when he sobered up, and I drove him away from my wagon, and he was left stranded at Brough Hill. I don't know how he got away and I didn't care, but I wouldn't have his company no more. That was Lancs of Shipley and that was the end of him, with me anyhow.

There was a stopping place for many years outside of Barnsley, and we all used to stop on it, and it was all ashes.

And the collier boys used to come and play football on it, you see.

Well at one particular time they was having a game, and the ball kept going over the Gypsies' tents and wagons and annoying them, you see.

And eventually it went over so many times that one of the Gypsy boys claimed it, and of course that stopped the football.

But a collier boy was picked to approach the head of the Gypsies for this ball you see, and this is how his story went, in Yorkshire you see:

He said: 'Now ah went across to the tent and ah seen a fellow and ah said: "Where's bloody king?"

'He said: "You'll find king in that tent yon!"

'And I knocked on the tent and I said: "Where's the bloody king?"

'He said: "Here I am!" and popped out of this tent, oh, a bloody great fine curly-headed copper-coloured fellow about six foot three. And he said: "Now, my son – what do you want?"

'I said: "Well, King, we've been playing football here for year in and year out. I know the ball has come over in your camp and they've kept it two or three times and they've thrown it back. But we've lost it for good this time. It's a new ball and we can't afford to lose it. And I wondered, King, if you could get it."

' "Well," he said. "Aye – I'll do something for you, my son."

'So this bloody king he put his fingers to his mouth and he whistled – and in two seconds the whole bloody tribe was all round him.

' "Now then!" he said. "Whoever's got this ball I want you to give it to me!"

'And in a second this king had our ball in his hand!

'And I said: "Thank you, King!"

'And I'm just turning round to go away, he said: "Here, my son. If ever you get in trouble with the Gypsies again in your life just show them that!" he said. And do you know what it was? It was a bloody bent hawpenny. And do you know, I can go amongst any bloody tribe of Gypsies now and show them that bent hawpenny and I can have owt to eat and drink with them – hedgehog pudding or bloody dog broth – owt you like!'

Now then there was an old horse dealer named Will, who was called one of the forty thieves of his day. And he was on his death-bed, and one of his children sent for the nearest parson to say a few words of comfort to him on his last journey on earth. So the parson came along, and told him there was still time to repent; and if he was willing to ask for forgiveness and pray the parson would ask the Lord to help him.

'No,' said the dealer. 'I have been told many times where I shall finish up, when I die, and I'm going where many of my pals has gone before me, and I shall be well prepared for the journey.'

When the parson left his bedside, Will sent for his daughter, and he asked her to bring a pencil and paper as he wished to make his will. As usual he couldn't read or write. And the following was his last will and testament:

'On my death the following articles must be placed in my coffin: Six strong halters. One lunging rope. My docking iron. My twitch. My old whalebone whip. And some dope' (laudanum).

Well, he died shortly after and his will and wish was carried out to the last item. He, of course, went to Hell. And he was at once tantalized by six young devils with horns and long furry tails, and when this first session was over they let him rest awhile, but they told him there was more to come.

But he was more than ready for them next time. He got his halters on the six, put each one on his lunging rope to stretch their necks a bit, tied 'em up to rings on the wall and got his whip and flogged the ears off 'em. Then he gave 'em a dose of dope and put them to sleep and got his docking iron and cut their tails off short.

Along comes Satan's second-in-command – and he was

shocked at the sight he saw. At once he hurried off to old Satan to come and see what had happened to six of his best imps – how they was disfigured, and Satan was shocked, and he ordered a court of inquiry, and the old dealer was questioned. And Satan asked him what his occupation was in the last world and with pride he said he was a horse dealer. Satan at once made an order to his staff that the old dealer should be shown the gate and that, in future, no one of that occupation should be allowed inside the gates of Hell.

Now where *do* horse dealers go when they die?

Appleby Fair in the Nineteen-Fifties

(Tales of Old-Time Dealers, Past and Present)

In Appleby Fair – they all know the date
It's the Second Wednesday in June, we've never been late.
From the Archway to the Quarry, to the White House up the
   Hill
From all round the country we're getting them still.
There's Bow-tops and Trailers, Accommodation and Tent.
And a Whoopee or two that someone's borrowed or lent.
Both sides of the road – right up to Long Martin
Horse Dealers and Travellers are having a party.
Scrap Merchants, Licensed Hawkers, Tatters and some more
There's Scotch and some Irish, and Welsh Travellers galore.
All has come to this Fair, to have a hell of a do –
There's Piebalds and Skewbalds and other colours too.
For the prices they make here rules the price for the year,
And on the cross roads, where the Quarry is near
There's old Tom Lister – claims his pitch every year.
You can hear him asking profit, on horses cheap and dear:
Old Tom's a tradesman – you may have no fear,
And he'll still be at horse trade later on at Yarm Fair.
And there's old Bob Farrar, who every Traveller knows
Who has travelled over Old Stainmoor in sunshine and snow.
He's still having some trade, and he takes on all comers
For his horses look good, in both winters and summers.
There's his pal Old Joe Vary, with his cobs on the corner,
He's just sold two spotted cobs to Stockton Bill Warner.
Joe Nicholson's bought four cobs from the Barks up the hill,
He thinks he's done well – but I think he's done ill.
He's sold the best two to Bob Harker to earn just two quids
And now he's left with the other two and they're very bad
   widds.
Now there's old Watson Dowse – the man we all know
Will deal for a horse or a pony – or even a sow,
He'll buy a lame duck, a dodge beast, in fact owt

And he's a'walked miles to buy a dog or a goat.
Good luck and long life to old Watson Dowse –
He must sell what he buys or he'll have a full house.
There's old Isaac and Dan Buck, they've just taken off –
They've left the Fair early – for Appleby Trot.
The Handicapper's given their horse just ten shouts –
And Dan disagrees while old Isaac just rousts.
There's old Gypsy Benney, he's as deaf as a post
Having trade with his son Jimmy for a little coloured colt.
There's Fred Pick with a trotter that's going great guns –
He will race for a hundred – or a bag of stale buns.
Jim Mouncey and Captain Simpson are never far apart
They've just charged a man for an old Bradford cart.
Not forgetting Sonny Shaftoe and the boys from Newcastle
Here having trade in the hustle and bustle.
There's old Reuben Wilkinson – he's never missed this fair –
His regular customers come every year.
Dave Howard from Castle Douglas, with sons Downy and Joe –
They're well known in Scotland, and further South too.
Not forgetting Downy Howard from Preston as well,
He's one of the few here with blood horses to sell.
John Buck with his wagons – he comes every year,
From the fairs, and the green lanes in his native Yorkshire.
There's Tommy Gaskin from Doncaster who paints wagons so
    well,
And Jimmy Berry who's as good, if the truth we're to tell,
And these two are painting a wagon or cart
And their results will be seen this year you can bet,
To brighten the scenery at Appleby Fair.
Now Bill Brough and his brother, Mike, are sure to be there
They have plenty of harness, and wagons that's nice,
With horses to fit them, and at the right price.
And if you find a bunch of ponies, looking sleek, fat and well
You can bet they belong to old Gordon Boswell.
And now the Fair will soon be over, and will come to an end.
The Cops are getting needled – they've had enough of my
    friends.
A Soldier's Farewell – and the Dealers don't care –
They'll be moving off soon, but will be back here next year.
It's Thursday – we must go, leaving relatives dear
(Where else could we find them, save Appleby Fair).
O'er the moors we will go, come sunshine or rain

Up North

And we'll just call at Brough, for to shop there again.
Some goes to Scotch Corner, and some to Smallways
To wash up, and clean up, before going their ways.
But many's now lying in their last resting places,
And the rest'll have to follow – you can bet your belt and
    braces.
I forget – so will I – I'm almost seventy-five –
I'm living on a cover-note – it's above the allotted time.
But my father lived to ninety-seven – I might just live to ninety-
    eight –
Before I leave all my pals, and seek Heaven's Gate.
And when that time comes I hope to meet the old Dealers there –
And I hope they have a place to take me to as happy as Appleby
    Fair.

The Horse Trade

But with the horse dealing – as time went on I got so as people used to rely on me. They would rely on me to suit them with a good horse, and give a man what he wanted.

In Leeds, when the discharged soldiers was coming home, they were getting a government grant for sixty or seventy pounds to buy a coal lorry, and set up a business. Because they were all keen on hawking coal. You could buy coal at the pit-head at nine shillings a ton, and go and get a load of coal and hawk it with scuttles, and sell it in stones, because that was how times was in the Depression: people could only afford a little at a time.

So a man would have a scuttle, and scales, and sell a stone of coal for fourpence, and that ton of coal would realize some profit for a clear day's wages.

So you would get your government grant of seventy pounds, and I would sell you an old coal lorry and an old horse to pull it, and a set of scales and twenty bags, and the whole turn-out would come to fifty pounds. Well I would get that cheque from the government, and you'd either get your turn-out and I'd give you twenty pounds – or perhaps you didn't want a coal lorry – you just wanted seventy pounds. Well, you'd say: 'I don't want the horse and lorry – how much will you give to get it back?'

'Well, I don't want it,' I'd say. 'I've just sold it to you. The most I can do is give you thirty pounds for it.'

'Ah well – give us the money!'

And I'd advertise it in the paper again, and someone would come along. Government grant. Seventy pounds.

'How much is that lot?'

'Well, fifty-five pounds.'

'Well, good enough. I'll pay for it with this grant. But I don't want it. I don't want the horse – I don't want the lorry and scales. I just want the government grant. You buy it back again.'

He'd want to settle for a fruit stall, or something of that kind. But it was a way of getting this grant. And I certainly had my share of this business.

But I left Yorkshire after a time, and I come down to Brig Fair, which was a very good horse fair at that time. And I was just coming into the Fair with my wagon, and four horses, and a dog, when the police come and said to me: 'Do you know any Boswells here?'

I said: 'I don't. I know the name – what do you want?'

'Well,' he said, 'if you happen to see any of them ring through to Skegness: the mother is between life and death, she is dying.'

It was the biggest shock of my life.

I got a place to pull my wagon, and I tied my horses up, and I was expecting my brother Lewis and Josh with some horses. They come in the Fair soon afterwards and I said: 'Mother's supposed to be dying. We've got to ring up home to the police station.'

I rang up the police station – got somebody belonging to me on the telephone, and they said: 'Mother's unconscious and wouldn't know you. You'd better come home as soon as you can!'

So I didn't know what to do with my four horses. Brig Fair was next day. So I said to Josh: 'Let Lewis make his way home – he's the youngest one so he has no ties.' So he made his way back to Skegness and he promised to ring the post office number at eight the next morning.

I was at the post office next morning and Lewis rang up and said: 'Don't worry, Gordon. Mammy's dead. She died at five o'clock this morning. Sell what you can and come home in time for the funeral. You can't do any more.'

Well you know I had those four horses at Brig Fair and I sat on the wall next day and I never sold a halter. I hadn't got the *power*. I hadn't got the power to talk to a man. It was the biggest tragedy that had happened in our lives, you know.

So I went and got a field with a farmer and I give him five pound to keep my horses, and to give the two dogs that I had bread and milk and to keep them, and I made my way to Skegness and Mother was laid out in a little wooden bungalow beside the two wagons on Cavendish Road and it was a terrible time.

Our family was there, a big coke fire outside, and well we was sitting round the fire. Poor old Father was there worrying, and talking and jabbering away about how she'd killed herself with hard work and so on, might have lived for years if she hadn't done so much work. All that, and my sisters and brothers all round and it was the worst time that we'd ever witnessed in our lives in our family.

Anyhow, Mother was laid to rest at Skegness and I went back to Brig and I thought: 'Now I'll travel down to Skegness for a few weeks.' And I got my wagon and horses down to Skegness and I found a gentleman that wanted a wagon and I sold my wagon.

So I had no home – only with my brother at the café, and it wasn't long before I bought another wagon, and I kept my best horse, sold two horses straight away in Skegness for landau horses, and when things settled and got into their stride again and Father seemed all right, I said: 'I'm out of this again – I'm up North!'

And away I went back to Yorkshire again.

Went back to Leeds and had more horse trade, and then I went and played about Wakefield. And then I got a house there, and some stables, and had a fair time.

And I bought a little slaughter-house, and got it licensed and I used to kill a few horses and export them to Belgium. And then I began to get live horses and cobs, and send them across to Ghent, when they stopped the dogs working in the milk carts. And I'd get pit ponies for this trade – and they was good to find at that time – and I could take ten or fifteen or twenty, according to the money I had, take them over in the boat from Goole, get them inspected, pay dock fees and veterinary fees, and land 'em at Ghent. Take 'em off, keep 'em for twenty-four hours for the veterinary test, and then take 'em to my salesman: a fellow called Paul Col. Nice fellow.

Paul Col seemed a Travelling breed of people, who was very wealthy. Very, very good horse dealers, and sausage manufacturers as well. Manufactured horse-meat sausages during the war for the German army. Had a very big factory.

And that was a time when there were lots of Gypsy people staying along the banks of the River Ghent, and any time I had during the sales of my ponies I'd get Paul to hire a taxi, and take me out among these people. And I tried to make myself known to them, as a Gypsy, and they was a lovely and good-looking lot of people. They wasn't all French Gypsies, or Belgian. There was some other nationalities. Because I think that with the war, you know, they'd been driven out: and they'd intermingled with Gypsy people of other countries.

But the most Gypsy people I ever met over there was when I used to go to Brussels market on a Friday, and it was full of Russian ponies at that time. You see, it was that five-year plan of Russia: they was left penniless – we deserted them – and they started their five-year plan you remember. Everybody had to work for the State and the country. And they had timber-drugs, and they was bringing timber from Russia to Amsterdam and Rotterdam. Convoys, oh, long convoys, of very crude timber-drugs, with slices of trees for wheels patched with pieces of iron, and cross-timbered. And the hub was just a hole through the slice of a tree, on a wooden axle, and a big wooden pin through to hold it, and a bucket full of bear's grease to grease the axle with, you know. And there might be as many as forty little ponies pulling one timber-drug in a single line.

And when they got to the docks, whichever docks it was, they would unload the timber, and they would save a few of the fittest of the ponies to take the empty convoy back. And they would put the rest in Brussels Market on a Friday.

Well, I would spend on these what money I had drawn in French or Belgian francs for my horses and cobs. I'd spend this money on the Russian ponies, because I could see they were a suitable pony to sell for pit ponies back in England. And I'd bring them back to England, in the same boat that was chartered, you see: I could get them on the same boat at the same rate and pay when I got back to England. And I could turn them out and 'lose' them for a while, until they got brand new.[28] And then they was sold either to private customers, or to the pit man to go down the pit.

And, in Brussels, there was some dealing men, Gypsy men, that used to be at the big public house near the market. The women and children would be sitting on the steps drinking. The men were long, some of them with spurs on – well dressed, good-looking men. For they was Gypsy people: they'd be more than one nationality: some were Hungarian, some German, might have been Italian Gypsies. I don't know. But it was an assembly place for dealing men to come and buy these ponies. And eventually the market used to fade away and you couldn't find many ponies at the end of the day. It was like a *sea* of ponies, used to be accumulated for weeks before, you know, with these convoys of ponies coming, and being fed in the pens. But when I used to talk to these people, with an interpreter, he used to tell them I was a Gypsy too, and I used to tell them how we built the tents and so on. I would have liked to have gone with them – you know they was a very likeable lot of people. But I still couldn't afford to be with them long enough: to forget for a little while, and it was back to work again, looking for that livelihood.

And I took a nice bunch of coloured ponies over there. I had an order: Hagenbach's Circus was in Ghent at the time, and it was a big circus, and I used to go to it and I got introduced through a Belgian man to one of the young Hagenbachs, and he told me to bring some nice ponies across and I took some over and I sold them to him.

And it got so that I had a nice lot of money on me.

But I didn't know about the money crisis.

The banks went wrong, and it came so the franc was worth nothing. The French franc went to three hundred and four hundred to the pound. And so I could only come home, and bring this money home, and I put it in the bank. And the manager said: 'Well – it can't stop like this. It must settle down some time!' And even the bank manager didn't know what it was going to do.

But eventually (and I know because I *paid* for it) they stabilized this money at so many francs to the pound, so many belgas to the pound, and out of all my lot – and I had in the region of two thousand pounds, which is what I had earned in this trade in three years – and when I drawed my money out of the bank I had about fifty-one pounds left!

And that put me right on the floor.

I hadn't got enough sense to think that if I'd gone to Belgium and lived with my money it would have been worth something – but over here, in this country, it was worth practically nothing at all. But I was just a Gypsy boy. I wasn't supposed to know all that. Because other big dealing men, they didn't know it. They lost money at the same time. Big exporters of horses. I was only following my leaders.

So I was right on the floor – I lost everything.

Now this was the time of the transition from horses to tractors, and I knew that I would partly have to leave the horse trade for other commodities, and it was a good thing I did. I had to start going into other trade, into the scrap trade. Because the average horse dealer was an efficient man, but a one-track man if you can understand. He just knew his standard of work and he never went off the side one way or the other. He just kept to his horses. He didn't want to *know* anything else. It was his living. He couldn't take to another life.

And I still couldn't keep my eyes off an old cob, or a horse, or a set of harness. I couldn't forget my horse and harness because I was *efficient* at it. I knew the trade through and through. I knew I had partly to leave it though, to get my living at other things.

The real horse dealer – and I term myself as a horse dealer – is a man who can totally live off the end of a whip, with his judgement to be shot at at all times – and his salesmanship. I had to go on with horses.

And I started travelling the fairs again. I took to the roads again, and the horse and wagon, and buying and selling horses at the big fairs.

Brough Hill Fair was recognized as the biggest in the North, nothing but illness keeping any Romany away from it. It was the meeting place of all our people, and certainly a fair attended by dealers from all parts of the British Isles.

Travelling up the Great North Road in the early days with horses and wagons was far different to the present time, with no heavy motor traffic – hours would pass without a car being seen and then only a 'T'-type Ford travelling at fifteen miles an hour. The roads were granite or stone, narrow too, though the grass verges were wide and plentiful.

The first stop would be Boroughbridge: usually the back road on the hill side of the town. The next day it would be Catterick Green where we would pull all the wagons together, light a good fire, and keep going till the early hours of the morning. The accordion would be played by Dover, the son of Noah Young, and the girls and boys would dance and sing. The people of Catterick would gather round and enjoy themselves too: they knew where we were heading for and looked forward to this yearly affair.

The next move would take us to Scotch Corner.

Where the big hotel stands today there was a very small farmhouse, and here we could buy eggs twenty for a shilling and fat hens at ninepence or one and threepence each.

We would then move over the Great West Road to Bowes Moor where a similar night as at Catterick would be passed. The next day would take us over Stainmoor, considered the roughest road in the country for horses in those days. It was a single cart track where in places big rocks faced the horses and wagons which they had to pass round. In places there are still pieces of the old road to be seen today where it has been by-passed by the new.

On to Brough Village, where water, bread and flour were

bought – and the bakers here did a roaring trade and soon sold out.

Then on to Brough Hill, where a city of wagons, carts, accommodations[29] and tents, belonging to all types and classes of people, assembled for this fair. There could be found on this hill Romanies and Travellers from England, Wales, Scotland and Ireland.

On the hill we had our own site on the Warcop side, just through the gate against the wall, and I noticed that for many years this site was never used by any other people than the Romanies – the women using their tents and wagons for their palmistry business during the Fair.

Trips would come from Blackpool, Morecambe, Manchester and Lancaster and business was brisk. Hands could be read by real Gypsies, and I have seen as many as forty families, all Romanies, along this wall with their palmistry tents.

I have often seen the late Lord Lonsdale take his walk in front of the wagons and tents, and he would have a word with most of us. He loved a good lurcher,[30] and there was always plenty in those days among the boys. He had to listen to many a tall story about the dogs' wonderful feats in coursing, told in the hope of his parting with some money. I do know that Terence Lee sold him a dog, a good one, for eight pounds: then a big sum money for a dog. For many good-looking but useless ones the standard price was a bob and a pint of beer.

It was at Brough that I first met my Uncle Herbert Whatnell with his wife Bertha and his family: Willie, Ruebena, Janie, Dorothy and Adelaide. They had just landed in England after being in Ireland for many years. They, with Samson and Wilhelmina Young, had been in Scotland that summer taking part in a film being made on Lord Atholl's estate with Victor McLaglen starring in it. The film was called *The Romany* or *The Children of the Caravan*.

Here also was my first meeting with Oliver and Julia Lee and their family: Relli, Lilly, Mena and Kissie. They were a well-known family in the North and old Julia was delighted to see me, because her father Bowie, or Bohemius Boswell, was closely related to my grandfather Silvester, and whenever she met anyone connected with her as I was she didn't forget to let all in her hearing know it. She treated me like the homecoming of a prodigal son, for although I had my own wagon on the hill at the time I had to stay to supper with her and her family. The menu was roasted hedgehog, for she said nothing could be more fitting for such an occasion as this.

The fat from the hedgehog was allowed to drip into a tin under the spit and was later sold by the old Romany women to *Gaujos* for hair oil, and was also recommended as a cure for deafness. It was inserted in the ear with the eye of a bodkin, for a hedgehog's fat never sets: it always remains in the form of a thin oil.

Life then for young Romanies and Travellers was a happy time. Round a good big fire, dancing and singing would go on well into the early hours of the morning, accompanied on the accordion by the well-known Pat Lee, a good musician who specialized in reels and Irish jigs. It was said that his music was the cause of most of the marriages among young Romanies in those days.

Future partners were also found at Appleby Fair or Brough Hill: the news of elopements[31] would usually be soon after either of these fairs, but Brough Hill had the majority – perhaps October moon and stars were more useful these occasions than June!

When all this was going on, the men would be having their trade. Some would sell their wagons or exchange them for anything else on the hill which they needed for their betterment.

When I was with Amos Boswell and William Noah, I was the only one at that time who could count money correctly, so I acted as clerk for the three of them. It was first agreed the amount of money they wished to lay out during the day, and the number of horses and colts they would need: generally about twenty-five to thirty. I would average the amount of money that each of the three would need to pool, and I would count out a bundle of fivers taking from each the same sum. Then handing half to Amos I kept the other to myself until needed later in the day.

Amos was the buyer in most cases, and my job was to soften up some of the Fell farmers with my tales: they had left their homes with a fixed price in their heads of what they intended to take home for their horses.

We usually convinced them different.

If they didn't take our price then you could bet all the tea in China they would later, because it didn't go well with anyone else at that time to finish a deal that we had started. Uncle Amos could tell a man off very sharply in those days and he was never let down in a spot of bother for there was many of us younger ones ever ready to do battle for him.

When we bought horses at this fair it wasn't possible to tie the young horses to the dry walls, so we didn't pay for them until the end of the day – and made the owners look after them for us and wait for their money. We did this so that our time was not wasted in looking after them ourselves.

After two days of trading we would then prepare for the return journey across the moors generally with a bunch of unbroken horses, for our next journey was to Hull Fair which in those days was a good place to sell these horses and colts to farmers in Yorkshire and across the water in Lincolnshire. The first days of this journey always proved a gruelling time for us – getting these colts across the moors to Bowes, teaching them to follow two working horses which would be ridden in front and another two behind. It took some hours before we taught the younger horses the job of following the others.

Some Romanies travelled light and made more speed than we could, but usually this journey to Hull would take eight days to complete. We kept the horses on the grass verge as much as possible to avoid them getting footsore, as all were unshod.

The fair at Hull was on 11th October, which allowed us two days' rest. We would pull our wagons on to the back of the fairground in Walton Street, and the business of the womenfolk was carried out in the front gardens in the street where they erected their tents for palmistry.

It didn't take us long at Hull to sell our horses and ponies, and after sharing out the profit money – which job fell on me – the rest of the week was spent as we wished.

The next move after this was to the winter stopping places: usually big towns such as Leeds, Sheffield, Bradford, Wakefield, etcetera. But Armley Brickfields was the headquarters of most. As my sole means of maintenance at that time was the horse trade I would move on to Yarm Fair, the scene of one of the oldest of English fairs, chartered as a horse and cheese fair. We pulled our wagons, carts and tents into the wide market place, with its old clock tower in the centre. This was the dividing line between the pleasure fair on the one side, and the Romanies and Travellers on the other.

I think, when looking back on the fairs held here, that the population of Yarm must have been the best-natured people I have ever come across. I have seen the smoke from big wood fires drifting up through the townspeople's bedroom windows and also other items of annoyance too numerous to mention, and it was a well-known place, too, for fights: it wouldn't be anything like a Yarm Fair if a fight didn't take place every few hours, for grievances had to be settled there and then. But the fights were short and fierce.

I used to go to the South for other fairs.

Barnet Fair, London, where it was held on its original place, that is, on the same side as Barnet Station (it's all built on now, and the Fair has been moved on the opposite side of the road and now it is down the lane half a mile from the High Road), this fair was the biggest hunting ground for all the villains in all businesses: Run Out merchants selling bags of money, Three Card merchants – find the lady, Pickpockets, and a gang called the Beenie Boys. There were droves of colts and ponies there. I had ponies there, and so did my brother Josh, with several well-known Lincolnshire dealers too. Old Moses Lee, a well-known old Gypsy man and his son Moses, always had some good Irish hunters tied up to ropes. Of course, when we were selling a wild colt on a long line, the more he bucked and reared, the bigger the crowd assembled, and the bustling of the crowd allowed the pickpockets ('at the Dip' we called it) to work without being under suspicion, and many in the crowd who had come with the intention of buying a horse or a pony found their wallets missing. Later several were there to play the part of detectives. When a person lost his lot, usually he was itching to report the matter to the police, of which there weren't so many in those days, and the supposed detective would take the matter over, and take notes and the address of the owner. Thinking his case was in the hands of the law, he could only wait to see if his loss was recovered and he wouldn't go to the real police.

All these things were going on while we were selling our cobs and horses. Barnet Fair was the fair of the year for the Cockney costers and others, and a general holiday for the Fair would last five days in those days.

The Beenie Boys, as we called them, were the heads of the gangs then, and would come and ask for a fiver or a tenner, according to the quantity of animals we were showing, for letting us work in comfort, or without disturbance as they called it, and we had to give it too. We never refused, for we knew we might be pulled into the crowd and britched as we called it. All this was the usual at Barnet during the nineteen-twenties and early nineteen-thirties.

Now the old Elephant and Castle auction and horse repository has closed down for good, and removed for space improvements, after being the headquarters in London for the supply and disposal of horses, harness and carts for generations. It lasted as long as the trade needed it, but for those of us living today who had connections in the horse trade like I have, all will remember the Elephant. As for Old Thomas Tillings' Bus horses and the London Omnibus Horse Co. horses – they all finished up in the Elephant Auction.

The Cobbler Joint

THERE was a period when I took to travelling the pleasure fairs. I worked the while-you-wait camera, you know, while my wife did palmistry work.

And I had a little – we called it a cobbler joint. The ball and the peg. We called it 'the mathematical problem'. There was a little stall about three foot six wide with a platform on it and a bar at the top, and a ball on a string from this bar. And in the middle of the platform a little pointed peg like a clown's hat. You had to hit the peg with the ball, let it swing. Of course nobody could win unless I let them win – and it was a case of having a gamble there. I'd give a man a few tries at this ball, and he'd knock it down for nothing until he got confident. And I'd say: 'Well do you think you could do it now?'

'I think so.'

'Well show me five shillings – I'll cover it with ten.'

And he'd have a try and he'd lose his five shillings.

'Well have another try. I'll give you another chance to win your money back. Show me another five shillings.'

The ball would go *round* the peg, you see, but I could put a spin on that ball to make it hit the peg. And if he *did* learn to do it there was another way I could make him miss – I used to say: 'Keep your eye on that peg – keep your eye on it!' and I had a wide-brimmed hat on, you see, and I'd just wipe the string with the rim of my hat and steer it round the peg. He couldn't win. Of course it's all barred from a fairground now, but it's a wonderful game.

It is clever because it mesmerizes even your students, you know. 'Yes,' they say. 'I'll have to work this one out.' And they work it out – 'central gravity' – I don't know what they call it – what is it? It's a very comical game. It's so simple to look at but can you do it?

And I give you three or four tries and I let you do it, and you feel confident. 'Well now,' I say, 'you're a monied man – you like a gamble, don't you?'

'Yes.'

'Well – five shillings and I'll double it with ten.'

And you do it just once. And you win your ten shillings. Then I put five down – and I win my ten back again.

'Well that's funny . . .'

'Have another go for nothing then!'

Give him that – let him win.

Then: 'Come on! If you want a nice gamble have a pound's worth!'

'No, I'll have half a quid.'

'Well alright – two to one on that and see what you can do this time.'

And I used to be at that lark at night-time, and work the while-you-wait camera in the day. People'd come out of the public house at ten o'clock and there's one or two a bit tipsy and they felt confident of theirselves with their money. I'd take them on at the mathematical problem.

Or else we had a game – Cover the Spot. You cover a spot with four pieces of galvanized sheets – they never would cover the spot. A little bit always showed. But with a sleight-of-hand I could show them how it was done. And I'd pick the sheets up and say: 'That's all you've got to do!' And they couldn't do it.

And the while-you-wait photographs – I'd sell them two or three in a set for a shilling or eighteenpence at that time and tell them not to let them see daylight until tomorrow morning. 'You'll be well satisfied with them!' But there was very little on them, and we was off the next morning when the fair was over and that was that.

It was *me* that mattered – self first, self second, and if there was anything left give it to self and I think that's the way of the world. And that's how I find other people has been living so I imitated them.

In the year 1927 me and Peterborough Jack – his name was Jack Elliott, a Travelling boy – we was travelling together as pals and we each had a trailer caravan at that time. Gypsy people, some of them, were then going over from horses to trailers – some of the first.

We decided to go on the 'Welsh run' as we called it. We started at Hereford Fair, and after that fair we went to Leominster and we pulled in at the bottom of the hill – the fairground was at the top of the hill. And we took a pitch for our two wives to do the palmistry business, and it was raining and the water was up to the floor of the trailer. And me and Jack was wet through.

So we got in the trailer – the best trailer of the two and we pulled our trousers off to dry them. And a boy come along with a handcart with these quart bottles of cider, and Jack said: 'Have you got any more of that?'

'Yes – a shedful.'

'Well let's have half-a-dozen bottles.'

So he sold us half-a-dozen bottles in a crate of this cider, and of course we was cold and wet and I said: 'It's no good drinking cold cider! We'll put it in a saucepan and we'll get the sugar pot out of the cupboard!' And we sugared this cider, and we kept drinking it because we liked it, and in the finish we was both as drunk as lords and I fell asleep with my trousers off. Peterborough Jack was sitting in the armchair by the fire with his trousers off and his shirt off to dry; and we'd promised to be up the hill at six o'clock to try and get an electric light on in this palmistry tent. But we was so drunk and we was asleep and it must have got six or seven o'clock and we didn't turn up. And Jack's wife come down and put her head up over the trailer door and she was shocked to find the two of us without any trousers and she couldn't wake us up. She was going to play hell with us, and anyway we was too drunk to get out of the wagon.

So they closed the tent down and the two wives slept in one trailer and they left us asleep with this drunken cider business in the other trailer.

And it was some days before we could get out of there because everything was flooded.

But we went in to Llandrindod Wells – to a lovely fair on a

hill. We got a few bob there – with the while-you-wait camera and the cobbler joint. And I had a little stall with a few dud watches on a green felt background. All of them was stumers – there wasn't one going. We used to clean them with Brasso to make them look well. And Jack had this spot game – the four plates to cover the spot. So we got a bit of a living there.

And we went on to Builth Wells and the fairground was in a quarry there and the Welsh boys at that time, they wasn't very pleased with anybody – it was in the colliery depression. Welshmen was very bad-tempered, they was angry; you couldn't get a drink on a Sunday. It was very religious and all like that. Still they'd come to the fairground but they didn't like money being taken off them. But Jack had a bogey with his spot game and somebody pinched two of my watches because he had lost about thirty shillings and he said: 'That will do to compensate me for my thirty shillings,' but he only got a dud one-and-ninepenny watch in the end, and we had a bit of a fight and lapped them up, but we had to pull down shop and get away.

The next fair was Risca, and we pulled the trailers in a little yard down the bottom of the hill and the fairground was at the top, so we built these two little joints – my cobbler joint and Jack had his spot game next to me at the top of the hill on the roadside.

And early on in the morning – it started early – up the hill came a little Welsh fellow with a blue melton coat on, a little bowler hat he would be about five foot two. And I pulled him into my cobbler joint, he lost five or six shillings – he couldn't manage my conundrum, my mathematical problem. I had a board, and on this board I had had printed: 'Teach me to win if I may win and if I may not win make me a good loser.' And if I had anybody that grumbled about losing a bit of money I used to show him this board and read it.

So anyway, I took this five or six bob off this little Welshman and then shoved him over to Jack. Jack claimed him covering this spot with these four pieces – he said: 'You do it

this and you do it that, try again, that's all you've got to do,'
he said. 'Show me five shillings and I'll give you ten.' So the
man put the five shillings on the table and Jack covered it
with ten shillings and of course the man tried to cover this
spot and he left a bit of red mark and he lost his job.

He said to Jack: 'Have I lost my five shillings?'

Jack said: 'Yes you have and do you want your mother
with you?'

Well he never said any more, and instead of going on to
the fair he turned and walked down the hill.

I said: 'That's a bogey, Jack.'

'No,' he said. 'He won't be.'

Well about ten minutes after he come back with two
policemen, big ones too.

And he pointed Jack out and they lifted him through his
coat – Jack said afterwards: 'I was halfway down my coat
and the coat was level with the policemen's shoulders' – and
they marched him down this hill. And I followed to see
where they was taking him, because I couldn't see a police
station.

Well they went beside a little chapel, and there was a little
brick building, stone building with a stone roof, and they
opened this door like a church door and shoved poor Jack
through. No windows.

And I could see inside there was a stone slab. It was a
mortuary.

I said: 'You're not going to leave him in there?'

The policeman said, 'That's his place. Now be off with
you.'

'I'm going to try to bail him out.'

'Are you a householder?'

I said: 'I'll find somebody to get him out.'

So I go up the hill, and Jack Evans was the secretary of the
Showmen's Guild of the Western Section at the time, and
we'd palled up with him, and I walked along and I said:
'Jack's inside. They've locked him up in the cold storage.
You're a householder – could you go and stand bail for him?'
I said: 'We've got no houses.'

So he said: 'It's a nice thing to come to the Secretary of the Showmen's Guild,' he said, 'to bail two lads with two little thieving joints!'

'Well,' I said, 'that's what you call them,' I said. 'I call them very suitable for the public at the moment in the mood they're in.'

So he tried, but they wouldn't let him have it.

He couldn't get bail – they wouldn't let Peterborough Jack out anyhow.

But the next morning at eleven o'clock they'd come to court in this chapel, and they were waiting for the magistrate. He was a little low-grown sort of a Welshman with a little beard, a man about fifty, and his little flat ears had been frozen on the mountains with the sheep – he was a little shepherd man I should think. His ears was all broken off in pieces, and a pair of rusty steel-rimmed glasses on, and he looked over to Jack, and when they read the charges to him about this, that and the other – he was charged – larceny – for obtaining five shillings by means of a trick.

So the witness got in – this little man got in the dock, and the magistrate asked him some questions.

He said: 'Your Worship – you know – I did not mind losing my five shillings, but I just said to this man "Have I lost my five shillings?" and he said to me: "Yes – do you want your mother with you?" Now,' he said, 'I did not mind in the least about my five shillings, but it was my mother. She has been dead for some years now, and also my two sisters, and it pricked me to the quick, Your Worship. It pricked me to the quick.'

And of course he found another witness somewhere – there was none there at the time he lost his five shillings, but he found one so *he* was a bit of a hook in my opinion, so we got fined eleven pounds and three pounds costs, or Jack did.

And of course we had to shuffle this up between us, and by the time we'd shuffled it we had but very little left. And when I got Jack out he'd lost about a stone and a half during the night in weight – what with fright and one thing and another. So he said: 'What are you going to do now Gordon?'

I said: 'We're going to fill the two tanks with petrol and we're going back to civilization!'

'Well,' he said, 'Where are we going?'

'We're going straight across into Cambridgeshire, to Ely.'

And we started off and we never ceased during the night but to pull in to a lay-by on the side of the road where we had a bit of a rest and got the children to bed, let them have a sleep, and got them up again and we were in Ely Fair next morning. And we built up again, and I walked about with my camera to take a few shillings, and it wasn't long before we got going again and was in the market once more.

Of course – funny thing – that the meanest of people looks for a gambling job. I've always found that out in life. A straight easy game they don't want. They want something where's there's a game of chance, and they gobble it, and when they work it out and find they're at the losing end of the business they can't take their medicine. And of course I can't help but laugh at such people like that. They should be like I say they should be – a good loser. If a man is a good gambler he must be a good loser. Without that he can't sail on, can he?

Of course we could let them win when we wanted. When they started losing two or three bob or a pound and like that, we'd let them have a win. And then, of course, it got them at it again, and then when they felt that they could win that's when we used to double the stakes and chop him off and make a whipping-top of him.

At Cambridge Fair one year we moved off the Common. We went down to Ditton boat races and pulled in the field there and the boat race was at the bottom and the students used to come. Well there was a man, Tippler White, the showman from Doncaster. He's dead now. He had a man that had trousers on one leg and a skirt on the other, a waistcoat on the left side and a lady's bra on the other side, half-man and half-woman. He was a fifty-fifty case, of course.

And of course these students was very rough, and they was determined to see what this client was made of and there was a hell of a fight on that ground to keep these students back because they was fine big fellows, you know. Anyway, the showman got this man away, half-man and half-woman – he had to get him away because otherwise they would have overhauled him.

And we had our cobbler joint as usual down the bottom end of the fairground to catch these lads after the boats had come by. And there was another fellow, another little fellow used to use a cobbler joint, from Leeds, called Louis Marks. He was a little Jew fellow, a wide-awake little fellow, and he took a nice few quid off some of these students.

In the night-time we had the old flare lamp, the naphtha flare, on our joints at that time, and these students come along and I heard one say: 'Oh there's that horrible little man! There's that horrible little man!'

And they got hold of Louis and we went to his rescue, but Louis got the flare lamp and he run at one of these fellows with the cap and gown and he set light to the gown and the man ran up through the field until somebody got the gown off him. And Louis set one or two more alight too.

But anyway they claimed poor Louis and they carried him down to the river and they said: 'Get hold of his arms and legs!' and they said: 'One, two, three!' and in the river he went among all the weeds and that like.

They pulled him out and put him in again: 'One, two, three!' and in again until poor Louis was nearly dead.

They dragged him out to the side and left him to us.

But Louis was like a cheeky one, he went and found out which college it was, and he went next day and identified these two or three, he put his wet filthy clothes on first, you see: he knew the ropes at Cambridge. He got the Proctor of the college and they made a collection for him and Louis came out with three suits of clothes and fourteen pounds. So he said: 'I won in the finish!'

That was at Ditton boat races.

But there was another time, when Stanley Thurston, on

the Common, would only allow my wife to be palmist on his
ground and my wife was doing fairly well, and at that time I
used to help her out with telling fortunes if she got too many
waiting. And some of the girls used to like me to tell their
fortunes.

And there was this queue of men, and I wanted Mabel to
hurry up, and I had a very nice kiosk tent with hands and
heads on, painted. And they, these students, kept peeping
into this tent.

And I said: 'You shouldn't do that! You should let my
wife work.'

Big fellows, they was. They said: 'Yes, Good Old Boswell!
Good Old Boswell!' They were shouting.

I said: 'Now don't. That's my wife in there – just pay respects to a lady.' I'm trying to keep to them and lap them up
to let us get to work because we wanted their money.

So one big fellow, he kept pulling the tent about – I said:
'Don't do that!'

He said: 'Are you trying to stop me?'

I said: 'I shall do my best.'

'Oh will you!' he said. 'Good Old Boswell!'

Of course I was no size to this big fellow. So he said: 'You
try and stop me!'

I said: 'Well, if you look in there and tear my canvas and
upset my wife, I shall try my best to stop you.'

And he went at this tent again to have a look at my wife
through the peep-hole.

Well, he just stood in the right position and I hit him
under the point of the chin and I dropped him like a
log.

But somebody kicked me up the backside on the last bone
where my tail should grow, and it struck a pain up to the top
of my head, and another one kicked me in the neck (I had a
lump on the back of my neck, oh, as big as an apple) and in
the finish – the lads could see on the dodgems that I was in
trouble, and one fetched a spanner and another a piece of
lead piping, and I ran after one student and I couldn't reach
him and I threw the spanner at him and I meant to kill him

f I could! I hit him on the shoulder and I believe I broke his collar-bone. It was said so.

And the next morning a very refined Indian student came o my wagon, and he apologized on behalf of the college for heir conduct.

Of course after that they closed the colleges – they sent hem away on vacation during the time of the Whitsun Fair at Cambridge and therefore we were quieter after that.

But by God they gave me a rough time: I mean some of he big fellows, they was very athletic fellows and brown brogue shoes on with soles three quarters of an inch thick! And I must have found the biggest pair that kicked me because I never had such a do in my life!

But I had to fight to defend my wife.

And of course there was a strip show at that time and the girl there – it was a posing show, and they took her out of the show – claimed her and carried her round the fairground on heir hands, you know. And then they raided a Noah's Ark and they wouldn't get off. I remember young Henry Thurson, he put a bit of extra speed in and threw many of them off that ride at that time because they just took possession – hey was a rough lot of lads.

But I didn't like Cambridge and the students, oh no! But with my cobbler joint, they'd come along and – 'I can't understand this and I can't understand that!' They'd go away and bring someone else back. 'Let's have a look at this! Have you seen anything like it?' And that pal would try to have his pal into it because *he'd* lost a few bob and he wants his pal to have a go. So the game was a good 'un. But when hey was lively, when they turned out of a public house . . . Or the young lads or a man would get a lady to do it and of course she had to suffer as well as the man because the man pays and that was alright and I used to get a few bob like hat.

Of course in the day I used to work my while-you-wait camera round the little kiddies' roundabout and pick out a nice photograph – baby in a pram, baby on a horse or a little motor-car on the roundabout. And I used to satisfy them and charge them a reasonable price – about sixpence a picture and that was alright. That was my afternoon's work. And perhaps Mabel would get a bob or two, fortune-telling.

That was our life but that was stopped in the fairground.

It was about in the year 'twenty-nine, when the Showmen's Guild stopped the palmistry business. They wouldn't allow the palmistry business on the fairground, on a Guild ground. Or camera workers, or palmistry, or this particular little ball and string game – what we called the cobbler joint.

ᗊ 11 ᗕ

Scrap

I REALLY went into the scrap business at Skegness, in between times. I would buy a big old car, perhaps; of course they were made of good aluminium, with coach-built bodies, and there was a bit of non-ferrous metal in them.

Engines was aluminium and you'd get some cars that had aluminium mudguards, and you got an original Vauxhall with aluminium brackets, aluminium housing and back axle. The gear box and sump was all of aluminium and sometimes the block. Aluminium was sixteen shillings a hundredweight.

Brass was fourpence a pound at that time. But it was according to the price of living: loaves of bread was twopence and twopence-ha'penny a loaf and you could buy farm butter for sevenpence a pound.

You learnt about metals: when you went to sell them to your metal merchant he would tell you. He used to sort this metal out – 'My son, that's brass . . .', but I knew what brass was through cleaning my father's harness. 'That's white metal.' We knew what white metal was from cleaning my father's white metal harness. And eventually we knew what gun-metal was because it was a different colour.

And we was always in with somebody that knew the job.

Travelling people – all old scrap men – 'Get hold of that, chip a piece of that – heavy brass. That bearing, that's not brass, my son – chip it like that – if you look at it it's a different shade.'

I can tell gun-metal, manganese, brass. I can sort the lot out today. I know what copper is and I know what bauxite is and I know what rolled aluminium is and I know what nickel is. I can tell the content of stainless steel – with what nickel content – if I put it on an emery wheel. You get the blue flame, yellow flame and your white flame. If I had any quantity of stainless steel that wouldn't take the magnet I know that there was more nickel in that than there would be in the stainless steel that *would* take the magnet. So there is two different prices. You become efficient at that.[32]

In about 1934 this country was in a bad state in my estimation, there was a lot of farmers going bankrupt. And scrap was worth nothing because I have known what it was to accumulate cast-iron stoves and so on from builders and have a big heap and be glad enough to put it on rail for eleven shillings a ton. But even then the idea was that the iron cost nothing but you could give money for a bit of non-ferrous metal. We could buy batteries at sixpence apiece and a twelve-volt battery for a shilling and when they were broken up they were only worth four pound ten a ton at that time. Sometimes we'd get a big storage plant in farmhouse cellars, you know, and that was better quality and we'd get five pound a ton for that. There was a lot of lighting plants before the electricity got about on the farms.

So I gradually built myself up.

And I was handy with wood, and I used to go to the wood yard when I was buying old cars – Morrises, Morris-Cowleys, Morris Oxfords at five shillings or seven-and-six apiece. And I started making little luggage trailers to go behind cars. There's some trailers in Spalding *now* that I made in 1934. I used to go to the builders and have a lot of wood cut out all one standard size for a little pig trailer with rails round it, and I remember that the sides and floor-boards and ribs used to cost thirteen shillings: the whole of the wood that is. And I used to take the front axle of a Morris and lock it in the knuckle of the king-pin, straighten it and split the track rod. And then bolt it on to the axle in two places and true it up, and leave the springs on, put a pair of soles on and a pulling-bar and build a little cart-trailer, if you like, with pig rails on. And a let-down tail-board with a pair of gate hinges on, and a bit of chain and hook and eye, paint 'em lead colour and shove 'em on the market and they would make four pounds. Perhaps a farmer would give us an order for a better one with bigger and stronger wheels – perhaps five pounds or six-ten. And I could make three trailers a week, with the help of my boy.

But I used to specialize more or less in going to workshops and machinery shops and looking for brass and gun-metal bearings and different things like that. But when you're in an agricultural district you've got to take what comes, you see, because there's not the commercial work about as there would be in an industrial district – Leeds, Bradford and north of Birmingham. So it's a hard district to get a living. It's thin. It's thin. So what are you to do?

So I started making these old trailers and buying old Morris cars and taking the wheels and axles off. I wasn't bothering about the other part of the scrap. But people come and see these spare parts laid down and they wanted a dynamo; they wanted a pump; they wanted a fan; they wanted another old engine – and naturally I sold them and they brought a living to me, and they taught me there was a living in spare parts.

And eventually it was a better living than what the trailer job was. Because then I started working in spare parts.

I got so much stuff in one place in Spalding that the landlord turned me out. He said: 'I'll give you one month to clear it.' I couldn't buy the place – I hadn't got enough money. In fact I didn't know the system *how* to buy it, really. So I went and rented another place and eventually *he* turned me out too. He started me at half-a-sovereign a week and he had thirty shillings a week by the time I did finish – every week he was asking for more money.

But at that time there was a lot of sales about in the Spalding district – transition to machinery again. And some people were going right out of business and they were selling everything. Well at that time iron was worth nothing – and I'm talking about 1935. Iron was worth nothing. You couldn't sell it. Wards of Sheffield didn't want it, Cohens of London didn't want it. Ridiculous price of agricultural scrap. So I bought what I could, I begged what I could, and I stored it away. And I was buying old lorries to get the engines out and the radiators and the metal and crown wheels were gun-metal at that time in most of the old lorries. Vulcans and Dodges and different things like that. And it kept on like that until in 1936 one day Wards' man came along, a traveller, and he said: 'You've got some scrap around?'

I said: 'Yes, I have. I've got some cast-iron and I've got some wrought-iron.'

'Well,' he said. 'If you put it on the rail you can have fifty bob a ton.'

Well I was working with a big old strong trailer and a big old car, a Buick car at the time – there was plenty of old American cars about – and I took the order. I thought I must have some money deposit first.

'How much do you want?'

I said I wanted a hundred pounds. So he gave me a hundred in notes and with that hundred I went and give it for a piece of land.

And I thought: now I'm independent of all those fellows that keeps kicking me out, I'll really go in for the scrap business. I thought: now that's it. I've got my own little place. And eventually I shifted, with my trailer, and I had a kitchen made about fourteen foot by fourteen foot and made myself comfortable on that piece of land, and eventually the old lady died next door and I bought her house.

I gave eighteen hundred pounds for that, and I bought the house and the orchard and a piece of land across the road.

And I stayed on until I had a wonderful business.

During the war (Second World War) I was registered with the Ministry of Transport, because if you wanted a new lorry at the time of the petrol shortage, if you wanted a new lorry you couldn't keep your old one. It had to be turned into produce, that is broken up for scrap to be melted down again, and you couldn't get your petrol until I'd signed for your old lorry to come off the road by me. But I was forced to cut that old lorry up into produce, you see, and send it up.

And then I had Lord Beaverbrook's scrap that was got in the metal appeal. They used to send it to me from the Women's Voluntary Service. I used to clean it, segregate it –

all the iron that was in it – weigh the brass and the aluminium, and the Ministry sent me bags and I laced it up and filled in a lot of triplicate forms and that like, and I eventually got paid for it by weight.

And of course we used to have some silly business with some of the Women's Voluntary Services during the war, you know, with this metal appeal. People sending from shops new aluminium saucepans, kettles and all like that, sending them to these Women's Voluntary Services.

People ringing up from Grimsby: 'Mr Boswell, are you registered with the Lord Beaverbrook Appeal?'

'Yes I am.'

'We've got an awful lot of metal, you know, here. We've got three or four bags of metal, saucepans and kettles and things. I wish you'd fetch it.'

Well they rang up three or four times and I couldn't go to Grimsby, ninety miles, for three or four bags of metal off these old ladies. And about the fourth time they rang up I said: 'Have you got an Air Force anywhere near you?'

'Oh yes, we've got a big Air Force here.'

'Well, will you go to the Commander-in-Chief and tell him that I said that he can deliver it here for you.'

'Oh can he? I didn't think he could you know. Oh can he?'

I said: 'Yes, we get that down from Sleaford and Cranwell and different aerodromes round here,' I said. 'They work with the Women's Voluntary Service.'

'Oh thank you, Mr Boswell.'

Well they rang me up again and said: 'That lorry is on the way, next morning.'

And a big Air Force lorry come, with high wheels too, a sergeant, corporal and two men, with four bags of aluminium and a weight ticket. I weighed it and gave them a receipt for it and the whole weight of the bags weighed four stone! And they'd delivered it from Grimsby in this huge lorry! And do you know these ladies when they accumulated anything they used to send it by Air Force – it's the truth.

And when the invasion scare was here, was about Lincolnshire, there was road blocks put all over the country, you know, this being the East Coast of England.

And one day there was a lot of troops stationed about here – anti-aircraft squadrons and so on – and a staff officer came with another officer and a sergeant-major and come into my yard and I had a lot of stuff.

He said: 'We want all this stuff here. We want everything.'

I said: 'Can I get compensated for this in the future? What's to be done? This is my livelihood. This is all I've got in the world.'

He said: 'What will you bloody well do if the Germans come?'

I said: 'That'll be a foregone conclusion if they do come. We shall have to receive them like what you will do. We shall have to do the same as what we did in the '14 war. We shall have to fight them like we did – and like I did.' I was a platoon commander in the Home Guard then.

He said: 'We don't want no nonsense.'

Well they pulled these chassis all over this part of the district, these lorry chassis, and they took cars as well that was on wheels and never gave me a chance to take the tyres off or the lamps or the batteries or anything else. I had five hundred vehicles at the time. They were laid about as road blocks. My yard was practically empty.

And I was collecting a lot of bottles of every description from the councils, and all like that, to sell as scrap, and I had a man name of Smithson to stack them up. And the army wanted them for Molotov bombs to fill with petrol. That officer – he went to all the chemists in town and took all the rolls of cotton wool and piled it up in the open in the middle of the camp and it rained and rained on them until all this cotton wool was a heap of muck. That was for 'Molotov Cocktails'. And they took thousands of bottles of mine, and do you know they was all broken and I never got a penny for my bottles and I never got a shilling for my cars and I was forced to pull them off the road when they told me, when they didn't want them any more.

I got them all back but they was stripped. Every tyre off,

every lamp, every bulb, everything. There was just a lot of work for nothing. And do you know, bottles after the war – oh, I sold bottles, depending on what class they was: whisky bottles, gin bottles, white and green bottles at, oh, about eightpence a dozen – well they had literally thousands of them off me and I never got one shilling. And when you went to buy a bit of cotton wool in the town you couldn't get it. It was a lot of nonsense.

Well, I lost about five hundred pounds I suppose. But I was still in the scrap business. I still made a living. I just had to take it as one of these things. And I thought, somehow I did think at the time that these people, the army authorities, knew I was a Gypsy. Somehow I felt it at the time, but then I felt it can't be! It's my inefficiency I thought. But still I hadn't got enough to back me up to play hell with the War Office you see. I still had to get a living.

It was in the second year of the war when owing to the restrictions on travel the Holidays at Home Scheme was launched, and I started with ponies and donkeys in the parks to ride children.

How I came to start in this business is, I think, worthy of relating.

About this time Murphy's, the Irish firm of cattle dealers, were sending hundreds of Irish beasts over to the big market towns of England including Spalding, and during one of these sales I said to Mr Paddy Murphy: 'The next time you send beasts to Spalding could you send me some good big donkeys?'

Paddy said: 'How many do you want?'

'Ten or fifteen – only let them be the best you can find in Ireland.'

'Sure now. You just wait till they arrive and they will be the best "cuddies" in all Ireland I will send you.'

Sure enough the next time Paddy arrived with more cattle he rang me up and asked me to meet him at the station, which I did.

Instead of bringing fifteen good 'cuddies' he had brought ninety-nine! All in trucks in the railway sidings.

I said to Paddy: 'Why didn't you send a hundred?'

'A hundred of anything is considered unlucky to an Irishman.'

'Paddy, how do you go on when you sell a hundred pounds' worth of beasts?'

'That's easy. We just give the buyer back a pound for luck.'

'Well, Paddy, I just can't do with ninety-nine cuddies.'

And he surprised me by saying: 'I didn't expect you could. Your idea has given me one. If you wanted cuddies sure there must be someone else who wants them too, and we will sell them by auction in the market.'

And so we did.

By the following week they had been advertised as real live toys for children in all the local papers.

They were a mixed lot. There were young and old, mares and entires, and there was more noise in Spalding that week with the music of the 'hee-haws' than ten sirens could make. The day of the sale came, and with it customers from near and far – fathers, mothers, children – all sitting around the cattle ring waiting for the sale.

This was a rare occasion for the auctioneer and he had no idea of the price of cuddies. But he said he had just sold a wooden horse for ten pounds.

The joke started when Lot 1 was offered – a nice donkey, for which bidding started at ten pounds. Someone asked if it was a mare. Paddy stooped down to look and just then somebody else said: 'Yes it is, and in full milk. The buyer is getting two cuddies instead of one.'

But the fact was it was an entire cuddy instead of a mare expecting a foal, and the bidding finished at twenty-three guineas. And the prices seemed to be around that figure for most of the others, all of them seeming to be mares when an inspection was asked for in the ring.

Many people who bought these donkeys had never been used to keeping any animal whatever before. They thought they would live in gardens and on the roadside and stay there without any attention, but they found that they would eat flowers, soap, paper, and chew the washing on the line and they all began to think differently.

Paddy was still laughing with his money, back in Old Ireland, but most of his customers were in a far different mood. Within the next fortnight I was the owner of another thirty cuddies at a price that fitted their many crimes and convictions in the owners' estimation.

In this way I started a business of riding for Holidays at Home, and on fairgrounds in the district. Instead of reducing the number I increased it, as for many weeks afterwards I found new foals being born. Eventually I changed to ponies for this work, and have used mostly ponies since. I worked these donkeys at King's Lynn Park, Wisbech Park and Cambridge Midsummer Fair.

I didn't get much rest at night, as, though the donkeys were always tied up in lines, there would always be a few people – mostly soldiers with their lady friends – who would wake up cold after sleeping out until the early hours of the morning, and would be bound to visit the donkeys. They would disturb them by pulling their ears (which all donkeys object to) and then the hee-hawing would start: one donkey after another. The resulting noise would either frighten the people away, or bring more soldiers and ladies to the scene, causing me to be up all night at these big fairs.

Later I found a remedy. I had one donkey that would do nothing right: he wouldn't allow anybody to ride him and he could kick a gnat's eye out, and bite too. So I tied him up by day and let him loose at night with a head-collar on and a leader dragging – so that he would be grazing near the others. When members of His Majesty's Forces came along they tried to catch him with the intention of giving their lady friends a cheap ride, but not many got as far as that with Neddy for he usually gave the soldier a pain in his tummy, and the more customers of this kind the worse Neddy became. He seemed to know what he was kept for.

No two of these donkeys were alike in their ways – all had different dispositions. I studied them from all angles, and came to the conclusion that they were just like people in many ways. Some were politically minded. At least some would work all day willingly. Some would only work half a day in earnest – the rest of the day they would either lie down or roll on a child on his back, or wouldn't go any distance without being led or driven. These were the trade unionists, I concluded. There were others who when a few old ladies came around to sympathize with them would drop their heads and ears and could give the impression that they were overworked and hadn't been fed for days.

And if anyone brought little bits for their favourite donkeys – I have known all the others to go on strike until I gave them some bread or something all round. I eventually made a rule for visitors to put their bits of food in a box until feeding-time.

Many people have asked me if I have ever seen a dead donkey – and the answer is: 'Yes. I have had several in my time.'

I believe that the donkey gets fed up with life in old age, because most people don't understand him completely.

The hide of the donkey is very thin, their skins when dried or cured being used for making kettle-drums and tambourines. I don't think the donkey can stand the wet and cold half as much as any horse or pony can – they come from warmer climates.

I had one donkey called Lumpy because he was so big. He eventually committed suicide.

We found him lying at the bottom of a field with his nose in water just above his nostrils. We got him out in time, put him in a float and took him home to the stables and I gave him a hot drink and eventually he recovered. We turned him out in the same field after a few days and later found him in the same place in the water– but this time he was dead. He had achieved his object. I came to the conclusion that he was fed up with life, and Holiday at Home, or was fretting for the land of the shamrock.

In the spring of 1944 I had been ill for some months and my doctor told me I needed a change and advised me to take a holiday. I decided to get my horse-drawn wagon ready and a governess cart to carry my family, with a Yorkshire flat cart on which to carry odds and ends which would be useful for the journey, and then make my way to Appleby in Cumberland for the horse fair.

This journey was two hundred and twenty miles by road, and I reckoned that I could complete this journey in about ten days' travelling time.

I had good horses for the job and we travelled on well, starting early in the morning, stopping for a rest and feed twice a day, and keeping on the move until late in the evenings.

We made Newark the first day, Doncaster the second where I picked up my old friend John Woods, with his family and his father-in-law Bob Adams who has since passed on. Old Bob decided to drive my wagon and two horses on parts of the journey, and not a mile was travelled without his stories of his past life and travels for there weren't many roads in Yorkshire, Lincolnshire, Westmorland and Cumberland that he hadn't journeyed in his seventy-odd years.

But he admitted that this journey was his best, for it reminded both him and myself of the days when we both had to travel seriously for a livelihood: a contrast to this journey intended for pleasure. I hadn't intended to do any business whatever, but after a few days I altered my ideas – I was feeling much better.

The third day's journey was a short one: from Doncaster to Wentbridge. The fourth day we made Boroughbridge and camped in the lane on the east side of the town which had been a stopping place for generations. Fifth day finished at Skeeby Lane, about a mile from Scotch Corner – a well-known stopping place. The sixth day ended at Bowes Green, but here we were soon told by the Military Police that we couldn't stay, owing to tanks and other government transport using the road, but we got a field to pull in for the night in the village.

The following day we became one of many families and Travellers of all classes moving on to this fair, for at Bowes is the junction for people coming from the North, through Barnard Castle, for the Great West Road. Here was a sight hard to be believed: for on this road were the bow-topped wagons of Romanies, the flat carts with accommodations on them and other travelling devices pulled by horses and ponies, belonging to the older generations of these people, and also Bren-gun carriers, Churchill tanks and other mechanical transport; and as we moved along to Brough Hill we found that half of it was covered with huts for ammunition storage, and on the other side of the road, being used for tank practice, was the hill which was used by my forefathers and others for hundreds of years, to turn their horses on during that fair week.

This has been forbidden land to the Romany and the Traveller ever since. It was a big blow, not only to the Traveller and the dealer, when the military authorities chose Brough Hill for this work, but also for the hill farmers for many miles around. For the farmer has stopped breeding the famous Fell ponies and the Clydesdale horse because there is no Brough Hill Fair of any size at which to sell his horses as he used to, before the fall of winter.

We did spend that night with others at the end of the camp just beyond the hill on the Warcop side, on a little bit of a green with a stream of fresh water running cold and clear beside it and a covert of ash and willow saplings on the banks of the stream, in contrast to the moors with their rocks and dry walls. It formed a wonderful resting place for ourselves and our horses too. The next move was to the end of the journey – Appleby.

We did it in less than eight days – a record, I think, during the war years, and for anyone attempting it with horses and wagons I doubt that it will ever be done again.

Well, when I got home I found my yard had got flooded when the river overflowed.

Spalding got flooded, and I went to the River Board, to Leopold Harvey which he was the head of it, and I said: 'My yard is flooded – there's five or six feet of water in.'

'Well,' he said, 'it's an Act of God. You can get nothing.'

Well,' I said, 'it's definitely ruined me.'

It had, because the water was over the tops of the cars. I must have had five hundred engines where the bank had washed away. The engines was all underneath it. I nearly lost four horses in a stable, and I lost a hundred and eighty hens because they was on their perches and this water come up so high they got their tails wet and it cocked them in the water and they was all drowned. They was fast in this big building and they couldn't get out, you see. I had four pigs drowned.

But anyway, Leopold Harvey he come down, and I told him such a pitiful tale, which was truthful, and he said: 'We want from the corner of your house ten yards of land to where that shed stands. We want to widen the bank and we want that quantity of land. We'll give you a cheque for a hundred pounds for that.'

Well that was good. They would put up a wire fence.

'And what about my engines,' I said, 'that's under that sand that's come out of your river?'

'Well,' he said, 'we'll give you a grant of seventy-five pounds.'

So I got a cheque for a hundred and seventy-five pounds. That wasn't so bad. And they sent a pump and pumped water out of the yard and they was working for a fortnight before they got it down to somewhere near normal. But it was still left with a pond at one end of it.

Well it went to 1950 and there was a slump in metals, and I had worked very hard during the war and I wasn't well and they come on me for a lot of tax, wartime tax, and I thought: why should I have this? And I got low in health and that like and I thought I had enough of money and I said: 'Sod it! We'll sell out!'

And I went down the town one morning, one Tuesday market morning, and had a bit of dinner with the auctioneer and I said I should sell my place if he found a customer. He said he might have somebody interested. And I didn't think there was one man would buy it, you know, because it was two houses and a big shed and a piece of land over the road: there was about two and a half acres really. And about a fortnight after this auctioneer rang me up he said: 'I've got a man coming out to look at your place this morning.'

Well I'd sacked six men because they was messing me about – you know: wanted this and that, and they wouldn't take orders from my sons and so on – all like that.

I wished a thousand times I'd have said I don't want to sell it but I was never known to call off in my life.

So he come down with the auctioneer and he said: 'How long will it take you to get out?'

I said: 'Two months but I'd rather *treat* you not to have it!'

He said: 'No. We'll just shake hands on that.' And we shook hands and we went up to the solicitor and signed the contract and that was the worst day's work I've ever done in my life.

Oh I got a good price: I sold it for five and a half thousand pounds. And then I called a sale for my surplus goods, got rid of as much as possible, and I went up in Yorkshire and I went to Scotland for a holiday.

I had two more trailers then. I had a lorry to pull one and a car to pull the other. And we went, took the family way up in Scotland for a bit of a holiday. And it went on, and I got back to Leeds for the Fifth of November, and the kids had saved up some money for some fireworks and I said: 'Well I'll find you a place to pull in – I'll go and pull in me old pal Arthur Catley's yard.' Well two trailers, two lorries and another car we had, and he said: 'We'll squeeze you in somehow!' I was going to a place to have a bonfire with my kids.

And I was pushing one of these trailers back and put a bar under the wheel and my back went out and I slipped a disc and I went unconscious and they tell me my tongue was almost hanging out of my head. And Arthur Catley went in the house and got a cupful of rum and poured it down me and made me vomit and I had the doctor to me and I was ten or twelve weeks on my back doing nothing.

And I didn't know what to do. I were walking about on

two sticks, and I went looking in papers and reading, and I saw that there was a place for sale at Killinghall, just near Harrogate.

Well, the kids, Julie and Gordon and Don, they was quite young – Julie's only twenty-six now and that was sixteen years ago – those three children I was looking at and amusing myself with, but I had the other boys with me as well; and I saw this Dales cottage at Killinghall, and I went and had a look at it and a nice little place with some stables and two paddocks, and I had some ponies left, turned out, and I thought I wouldn't sell them, and I bought this property and I had my ponies on this land.

I ran a bunch of ponies taking children for rides at Harrogate, and got the R.S.P.C.A.'s medal for the best-kept animals, and I went in for horse trading but didn't do any good. They wasn't the people I'd been used to dealing with. If you sold them a pony in the springtime when the grass was coming, when it was all gone they wanted you to buy these articles back at the same price they give for 'em, without taking into consideration the amusement they had had, and the price of ponies at the back end.

So I didn't get on very well, and I slid into a good game fellow and sold the place to him. The first man that come along. And I sold it to lose a lot of money. After about two years there I sold it to lose sixteen hundred pounds. But I thought: I'm living, I'm still alive.

But during that period – I think the reason why I didn't do any good – my wife was taken ill with yellow jaundice and poisoned blood stream and gall-bladder stoppage. She was already a diabetic. And really going there was the luckiest move I ever made in my life, because she was taken away immediately to Harrogate Hospital, and I had the best of specialists I could find to operate, and for a time she lay between life and death.

They did experiments; they asked if they would be allowed to experiment on certain things with her – it was only a fifty-fifty chance, but I thought I'd take that. And she recovered anyhow, and I feel that all I lost I gained because

I've got my wife still with me and she's attended to me night and day all her life.

And I travelled about for a while.

First I went to Esham, and I had some ponies on the beach there, and I said I'm chucking it, and I brought my ponies back to Cambridge – I still kept that pitch, you know, at Midsummer Common. Took me ponies down there and I didn't do any good – it rained – and I said I'm pulling into Spalding.

So I come back here and nobody had started in opposition to me, and the surveyor said: 'Well you can't have a scrap place in the town – the authorities wouldn't allow an obnoxious business like this in the town.' They said: 'Get somewhere in the district in the rural area, and we'll say yes, if you find a place.'

So I bought this.[33]

And, you see, I had my three boys, Lewis, Donnie and Gordon, and I said: 'I'll get the business back again.' And I got all my clients back again, or most of them.

The moment I got back I started searching all around, and I bought this and I bought that and fetched it on this yard, and eventually I sailed on and I had a better feeling. I got back where I belonged to.

I tell you people had my confidence when I left.

I never owed a penny when I was at Skegness. When I left Spalding the accountants did me up and I said: 'We'll pay all our debts.' I had plenty of money owing me although I had to put a few people in court and I got a cheque now and again for that, but I settled up everybody before I left quite good and respectable knowing that I might want to come back – or some of my children.

And I come back and there was just as good a feeling when I come back. People was just as pleased to see me although I'm saying this myself. I got the majority of my old customers back.

I've been in this business, well, in the business since 1934 in this town, and I've never been convicted of any crime regarding stolen stuff – which there's plenty of temptations, but I've avoided it. My boys is of age now. They've been warned in the past that it isn't worth it. They're ... careful. So they are held in great respect in this district – we're *business* people. They can trust us on their premises. We deal with like the Sugar Corporation, or some of the biggest tractor firms in this district, the biggest farmers in the district, potato merchants like William Dennis and Sons, of Kirton.

We get all the scrap off all the farms in this district; they leave it to us to collect it, and we weigh it, send the tickets to them with a cheque in it and that's beautiful. We've got the confidence of other people and other people have got the confidence of us, and I've lived for it and we've achieved it and I hope we carry on like this.

Machinery: I've got a guillotine, a German guillotine, we've had it for some years now; it's still good. It cost two and a half thousand pounds. Then I've got a mobile press with a diesel engine; it cost two and a half thousand pounds. And we've got two or three cranes, which they're redundant now because we've bought a mobile crane with a magnet on which cost in the region of four and a half thousand. And lorries: we've just renewed with a Super Leyland Comet which is only eighteen months old and which is a good lorry. On account of Barbara Castle, I've been caused to spend more money on one particular article than we've ever spent in our lives in the way of a lorry, because we've usually done our work with a ten- or fifteen-pound lorry, and they've gone up to three hundred, five hundred, six hundred, eight hundred – and now it's gone up to two thousand two hundred! And it's taken new working capital out and we feel we've been shovelling sand with a fork because the working capital is completely eaten up in machinery.

But I can't afford to give up. Because my boys is in business – it's their future and if they try and look forward instead of backward (like I've done sometimes), there'll be security for them as long as they work, but if they won't work I hope there's no more security for them as what there is for any idle man.

They *do* work. They're very good men – the best of boys. They don't want no clock to work to: when the light hours is there they're up in the morning and they finish at night-time. And I still go just the same with them but I'm hoping to lighten my load very shortly: it's too long to go in life – a seventy-four-year-old man working hard. I'm going to take things easy very shortly.

⁓ 12 ⁓

What Gypsy means

THAT's what I'm waiting for.

I will travel. I can't help it.

The moment I've got a weekend to spare now, or the week, or a fortnight: hook my car and trailer up and I must go and go, and stop on the roadside and go to a horse fair – it doesn't matter whether it's Barnet Fair, Appleby Fair, Topley Fair or any little fair, it makes no difference to me. I must go because I can see somebody attached to me: it's my life. It's all music to me, and without that this life is of no use at all to me. I wouldn't have lasted as long at this job as what I have done if I hadn't mixed it with my original life; without that it would have no meaning. I believe I would have been a dead man at this lark.

Because putting me in four walls and stagnated in one place to stick at it from Monday morning till Saturday night and having one week's holiday a year like the normal man does – oh, that would be absolutely punishment for me; it would treat me the same as what Pentonville or Dartmoor would be.

So I've kept my wheels turning whenever I could. Whenever there's been an idle weekend I've been off to Yarmouth to see friends there, or a bit of fishing. I've took Mabel, took my fishing rod and gone out here eight to ten mile and pulled up some fish – lovely, and she's made me a cup of tea and if I've only been catching tiddlers it's been lovely and I wouldn't be without that life.

And I still buy an old cob or a pony, or I keep a donkey. Because I like animals and I shall always finish up with animals. I don't care: a goat will do me as long as I can buy one; and if I can't manage with a goat I'll manage with a rabbit! It doesn't matter what it is, I must have an animal.

Because iron doesn't talk. Metal doesn't talk. You only

handle it to get the returns of it to have something to eat – three meals and a bit of supper. And there's no *music* attached to it to me – to metal and iron – to me it's there for a purpose to get a livelihood. And it's the only way I can get it, I expect.

And the moment spring comes and the grass is shooting through – like it is *now* on the sides of the road – fourteenth of February is coupling day for the birds and it was my father's day and it's my day. I must be getting a move on. I'll be straightening up things, levelling up the business so I can get away. I don't care where it is – it could be round the other corner, it's a change, and if I keep going I don't care where I go. That's life for me.

Or I go to Doncaster Racecourse in Leger week, or Appleby Fair, in Westmorland, in June.[34]

I must tell you a funny story about my travelling nowadays – and it's truthful and amusing.

I was pulled into a lay-by with a nice trailer, not a very big one – sixteen foot – and a good car, a Zephyr or Zodiac, and I was sitting on the bank having a smoke and up came a trailer, a gentleman with a trailer, a Sprite or something of the kind like that. And he had a flag stuck on it.

While his wife was cooking or getting his dinner ready he said: 'That's rather a nice trailer. It's a strange make.'

I said: 'Yes it is. It was made in Penrith. That's a special-made trailer – it's a bit on the heavy side, but it's comfort. You could live in it winter and summer.'

'Very nice trailer,' he said. 'What are you doing? You haven't got your flag up!'

I said: 'Well, what do you mean?'

'Caravan Association.'

'Oh,' I said. 'They won't let me in that association.'

'Why?'

'Well do you think you could get me in?'

He said: 'I think so. I think I could recommend you to get in.'

'Well,' I said, 'I wouldn't waste your time because I don't think they'd let me be in.'

'What on earth for?'

'Well,' I said. 'I'm a Gypsy.'

He said: 'You're not are you? You're not a Gypsy?'

'Oh I am,' I said. 'And I'm proud of my race. And a man who's not proud of his nationality is no man at all. I'm a true-bred Romany.'

'Oh, you're not! Oh you're not!'

I said: 'Don't feel nervous because you're in the same lay-by as a Gypsy. I won't hurt you. I won't steal anything you've got. Because what you've got is not as good as what I've got, so it's not a bit tempting, so rest your bones and have your meal in comfort. I'm sure I won't hurt you.'

'Oh,' he said. 'I'm not afraid of you.'

'You sure? Sure you're not nervous – with a Gypsy? Stay a bit longer. I'm in no hurry. Let's have a talk together.'

He said: 'Well, *why* won't they allow you in the Caravan Association?'

'I know – I've tried,' I said. 'What's wrong with me – as a Gypsy?'

'You don't look an average one. Probably you're a foreigner.'

'No I'm not. No. I'm Romany. I'm a Gypsy man. I've lived in England all my life – I was born in it. I've travelled every lane, every lay-by, every common in the country that's been worth going to. Can you say that?'

'No I really can't.'

'Are you enjoying your holiday?'

'Yes, and I'm hoping to.'

'That's right,' I said. 'Do you know you are just imitating a Gypsy with that caravan? Because we've had this for generations. Pulled by horses and now we've got motors and trailers. But I like to see people like you get trailers because maybe you'll learn something. It's men originate and monkeys imitate. Now you're not looking at me nice – you're not taking this medicine good.'

He said: 'How the hell can I? You're too much to the bloody point.'

'Well I'm used to giving it to the point when I get a chance because I have a cause to defend, and it's a very strong cause too and I intend to defend myself and my people. I'm like a man in the boxing ring when two men get together. It's defend yourself at all times and that's been me all my life and I've had to defend myself. And now I've lived to be in a position when I can tell you people I intend to put it on thick and heavy.

'Look at me!' I said. 'Look at me – as a man. You've seen a Gypsy today, and if you go further up this country you'll see a lot more. Go amongst them and find what they're like. You'll find that they're more entertaining people than what you are. Go and mix with a different class. Keep off your "flag camp" and your "caravan camp", and go and find a Gypsy camp and try your best to get in. They won't want you, but if you go with the right feeling and the right approach they will welcome you and you will learn something – something you'll be able to talk about all this summer and all next.'

But of course, when I travel now, with a twelve-foot trailer, or a sixteen-foot trailer, people – the police – think I'm a holiday-maker. And they leave me alone. If the police knew I was a Gypsy they'd soon be on my toes wouldn't they?

And you know I've always found, both on the road and in court, with a Gypsy the prosecution is nine times stronger than the defence. The Gypsy never says nothing until he's prosecuted, and then he rears up and he tries to defend himself – very hasty, very sharp, very sweet. He's only got a few seconds to do it. He loses his temper and he says what he thinks in his uneducated way. If he would have the patience to talk to these people, but without education it can't be put over. The show can't be put over where it comes to prosecution and defence. Against – that is – an educated man.

Because an educated person – I've always found out and I admire them for it – they can use less words. Put them to you in sentences and you've got it in a nutshell. But a man that's not educated, he's got to think and he's got to thoroughly explain himself in his way to find a few words to put together, and it's a long sentence, and therefore the educated man beats the uneducated at this job. So it's difficult, because the educated man doesn't seem to have patience, or tolerance.

Oh, but I would willingly go back. I would like to have my wagon and my horse and go back exactly to where I think were the happiest days of my life. Free from worry, free from troubles, live close to nature: see the rise and the fall of the leaf, the buds, the birds.

I've gone with the times as much as I could keep up with them. But they've been too fast for me, and they've certainly been too fast these late years.

But now I'm in the position that I am, I'm quite happy: all my family is quite comfortable. They can all get a living. I hadn't any worry with my children. They've not brought one moment's trouble on me or on their mother. I had five boys and two girls and have looked after lots of other Travellers' children too, in my time. And they are all doing well today. These are the happy moments.

My poor old father lived with me, in his own wagon, right to the end. He looked after himself. He wouldn't live in our house: I had two houses at one time, but he wouldn't live in one under no consideration. He said: 'I don't want to live up your stairs with four walls, and you go upstairs to the lavatory and you pull the chain, and when you pull it your rubbish that comes from your body passes through your pantry. You call yourself clean people?'

He wouldn't have no house. No.

I remember about eleven years ago – 1948 or '49 – the white five-pound notes was called in and I said: 'Now, Father – these white five-pound notes are called in and they've got to be in by a certain date.'

'Such nonsense, boy! Such nonsense!' he said. 'Go and mind your own business. You want to find out what few shillings I've got.'

'I know but they've got to be in by a certain date.'

But he neglected this till the time was up and after the time. I kept reminding him about these notes. I said:

'You'll never get anything for 'em if they're neglected much longer.'

And probably two years have elapsed, you see, so some old Travelling man come and see him, and my father said: 'Is it right – my boy tells me that these five-pound notes have got to be called in?'

'Yes, Algar,' he said. 'They should have been in two years ago.'

So one morning he come to me. He said: 'Well then it is right, you boy,' he said, 'that these five-pound notes have to be called in.'

'It's right and you've neglected it and you look like losing it.'

'Well can you do anything about it?'

'Well I'll try my best, but you're a silly old fool of a man.' I said: 'I'll go to the bank manager, and I'll tell him what a fool of an old man you are, that you've had these stored away and you've kept them secret from me, and will you do something for my father?'

So I took them to the bank, and I stated it to the bank manager that there was eighty-five pounds in five-pound notes and he said: 'Well leave them here, pay them into your account, and come and see me in a fortnight: we'll see what we can do for you.'

So I went back to my father. I said: 'Well I've handed them over, and the bank manager's told me that it'll be at least a fortnight before I can tell you anything different.'

Well every morning from then on he used to come puffing and blowing. 'Now my son, you millionette.' (He used to call me a millionette for a millionaire you see.) 'Now my son, the millionette, I want my few shillings. I want my few pounds. I've always been used to having it where I can lay my hands upon it and I want it.'

'Ha!' I said. 'But you're not having *my* few pounds. I don't know whether yours are good or bad there in the bank and you've got to wait a fortnight.'

'I tell you distinctly I want my money!'

He's trying to bustle it out of me!

'I'm not standing for your mistakes,' I said. 'You're going to be the loser, not me.'

And every morning during that fortnight my old father come to me: 'Will you go to that so-and-so bank and tell them – go to that bank manager and get my few shillings back. I want it and tell them I've been *used* to it!'

So, anyhow, every morning he just come up with a repeat of this, but he tried to squeeze it out of me with my money. But I wouldn't stand for it.

But at the fortnight's end I asked the bank manager. He says: 'Yes. Everything's alright. Write your cheque out and I'll pay it over to you.'

So they paid me this eighty-five pound in one-pound notes, and I took it to my father and I said: 'There you are! There's your money and you're a very lucky silly old fool.'

But he said: 'What did you get one-pound notes for: a bundle like that?'

'Well,' I said. 'I'll change them into fivers.'

'Aha!' he said. 'They might be the same as what you put into the bank belonging to me.'

But eventually he took my notes, and he used to keep this money in the end of his old fiddle box at the end of the bed, you know. That was his bank. And he always used to say before he died: 'Tomorrow, my boy, when the breath goes out of my body and the good Lord takes me, you'll find my few shillings in the fiddle case there, it'll be enough to put me away. I want you to lay me beside your mother at Skegness.'

I said: 'I'll take you if I have to take you in a wheelbarrow.'

He pointed to his tongue and to his heart: 'Is it from there – or is it from there?'

'It's from my heart – I'll take you there.'

Anyway, you know, my father had already bought his piece of ground beside Mother, and when he was buried there I had the stone taken up and his name putten on it. But my father was a very funny old client. He just had enough money to bury him with but that was all.

To the end of his days my father always read a verse from the Bible every morning, and in the evening he would pray, and he was very sincere, and very *loud* so that if you was anywhere near his wagon you could hear what he said, and this is a sample of the sort of prayer he used to say and I've heard him many times:

'Now, my Lord, I've come to the end of another day, and I just want to tell you that I've washed myself, and my feet is clean, and I'm ready for you to take me when you think fit, my Lord. I know – and you know – I have had a good innings. I have seen all I want to see, and it's not of much interest you know, my Lord. I have been to Ireland and Scotland in my young days, with my wife Athaliah. I've seen the hills and the beautiful rivers and streams, with the salmon and trout. You know, Lord, I've had rabbits and hares from the hillsides – and in Wales too. You know, my Lord, I've travelled in Norfolk, Suffolk and Essex, and bought a few old horses. And I'm ready for you to take me when you are ready, for I'm clean and washed for the Journey. I have told that boy Gordon, that millionette over the road, just what to do with me when you take me, my Lord, and I believe he will do it, I'm sure. I told him when the time comes to go and pick a well-seasoned piece of elm, one and a quarter inches thick, to make my box, and have it well pitched inside, and have a sloping lid on it so it will shoot the water off, and then take me to Skegness and lay me beside poor Athaliah. He has promised to do that, my Lord, and I believe he will. He is a good boy, my Lord, but a rank stark staring fool at times, my Lord. I have told him many times that when the breath goes from my body he will find enough money in the end of my old fiddle box to do the job, Lord. He has told me he will take me there in a wheelbarrow if he can't take me anyhow else, and I believe he will, my Lord. I have just walked over there a few hours ago and he showed me two horses he bought today. He said one cost forty-five pounds and the other cost fifty, my Lord, and I told him I've seen the time in my young days when I've had better horses in the shafts of my old wagon for two pound ten and four pound ten. What a fool's world this is, my Lord – I have had enough of it. I am tired. And I'm ready for you to take me when you think fit. I'm just going to play a bit of a tune on the strings of my old fiddle, and then lay my head down, and that's all I've got to say to you, my Lord. So good night, my Lord.'

A fortnight before he died he used to walk up to the Spalding Market on a Tuesday – it's quite a mile from my yard – he used to like that bit of exercise. And he used to cook for himself you know. He wouldn't live in our house. He wouldn't cook in it. He lived in his own wagon and he would buy a bit of steak – it was when the coupons was on – and he used to walk into a butcher's shop and he'd fancy one little bit of steak and he'd say: 'Just you cut me two or three inches off that!'

'It's on coupons, Mr Boswell.'

'Never!' He used to call them 'summonses'. 'I've got no summonses – I just want a little piece off there.'

And he would take it home and one particular Tuesday, a fortnight before he died, he bought some new peas and he bought his usual piece of steak and he made his fire outside and had a bit over the grid-iron and he would roast it on his grid-iron and he boiled his peas and enjoyed his dinner. He told me he enjoyed his peas and his bit of dinner. He used to lay back on his bed and perhaps have a sleep and a smoke. But he must have turned over on a full stomach and twisted his bowel, and I had the doctor to him, of course, but he was in pain after the first three or four days and the doctor put him in hospital and he was too old to operate, and I brought him home – he insisted on me bringing him home – and I put him in his own bed and I stayed with him night and day until he died. But he lived a fortnight.

I naturally done what I was told. He wanted a special coffin made for him. He had said: 'You go and pick a piece of elm, well-seasoned inch-and-a-quarter. And I want you to put a lid on it that will shoot the water.'

So I had the right lid, and then a smaller one put on it and a smaller one still – till it come to a point you know. I said: 'If you want I'll have a tent built over your grave!'

And he's there with two of my sisters and my brother in Skegness cemetery and I look after his grave.

My sons are good boys and settled in this business. But I've got one, Lewis, you see, one in the family who is a real Gypsy man.

He loves his stick fire, he loves his green grass exactly like me, he will never settle. I don't think so. I can't see him settling – he's not that type; he doesn't want to and his wife doesn't. So I think that's good.

He's married a Romany girl. Yes, a Smith. They've got two children, but he wouldn't, he wouldn't swap his home away for a mansion or any different kind of life. He doesn't want anything further. He gets his daily work and he's not looking for a fortune you see. He lives from day to day – yesterday is gone – forget it, tomorrow never comes – don't worry, today is here – use it!

And that's been my motto and that's his.

And whenever Lewis meets me with his trailer, or I go and see him if he's up, say, in Yorkshire, I'll perhaps go and have a weekend with him. I know he says within himself: 'Father's coming – we'll pull in here – Father's coming to such and such a fair . . .'

Lewis is the typical Gypsy man. More of a Gypsy man than anyone left in the family, and I think he intends to lead the life as much as he can and as much as he *dare*. Although that's difficult at times, even for him. But he'll turn his hand to anything. He'll turn his hand to a bit of scrap. He'll do a bit of tarmac for a garden path, or forecourts or something like that. He's a Jack-of-all-trades, if you understand me. He likes the Gypsy life. The roadside and the fairground. He likes a horse, he's a good horseman. He's got one or two for his kids, but he can't make it a business – he can't afford to. It's a luxury – occasionally. It won't keep you, will it?

He travels a lot. He'll perhaps move off to Penrith or Carlisle, he may have a few weeks up there until June spraying farm buildings if the weather's right. Or he may be at Morecambe, or the other side of Newcastle. If I feel I want a week or ten days – I'll go up and meet him, but you can bet your life he's somewhere where a bit of green grass is and he's got his *yog*[35] beside his wagon whether it's hot or cold. He'll wait until the cool of the day and he'll still have his fire.

He likes that and his children like it. They're not ashamed. They don't want to get away from the life. Yet they go to school. They wear these little badges, and they get monitors at school, and they're very intelligent. Lewis is like me – he's giving his children as much education as he can, and fill it in in the winter months, and then when summertime comes they've got to move, and if they're in a place for a fortnight or three weeks they send them to the nearest school if they can fit them in.

Yes, Lewis's little children will tell you he's a Gypsy. He's a Romany, a real Romany man. That's what his little Lewis will say. Little Duggie does the same. Little Jimmy – 'What are you, Jimmy?'

'I'm a Gypsy!'

And then probably these children will turn round and say to me when I tell them to keep quiet or something in the yard, or not ride their bicycle, they say: 'Gypsy – Gypsy – Gypsy Gypsy!'

Oh I like it – go on – carry on – keep it up! I like them to keep the word in the name – that is, with me. I tease them for it, to bring it out of them.

And then eventually they'll find out what Gypsy means.

I would like to travel the roads again
As I did in the days gone by,
With wagon and horse, and a few old cobs.
To feel in my pocket and count my money
In case I find a *grai*[36] to buy, or a customer for one of mine.
For something will turn up I'm sure of that
I'll find some trade somewhere or eat my hat.
But first I pull out here and rest my old horses
Where the willows grow yellow. I'll sure find some water.
And the grass grows so thick – there's no need to go further.
So I kindle a fire with ash twigs and stumps,
The kettle's on the prop stick, for I must have a drink.
I'm off to this brook to look for a trout.
I'll walk up the stream, against the tide, gently,
And just find a rock where I'm sure trout abide.
I've found one I'm sure! I'm up to my knees –
I'll just start to tiddle him as quiet as I can.
It won't be long now – he will be in my hands
He's feeling quite pleased with the feel of my hands
In a second my fingers will be in his gills
And all of a second – oh what a surprise –
He's out on the bank – and I've got my prize!
For he is a good one – he sure weighs a pound
And he'll soon be on a spit and stuck in the ground –
With the heat of my fire I'll soon have him brown.
But first I'll have a look, both ways up the road
In case there's a keeper, or the Law hangs around.
All things are quiet, so I'll sit down to dine
And thank God for the trout, and the good things around.

Appendices & Notes

Appendix I

Records of my Family Tree

My great-great-grandfather was called Shadrack Boswell,
the father of Tyso Boswell, my great-grandfather, and Cinderella Wood was Tyso's mother. Shadrack, my great-great-
grandfather, was a soldier, evidently in the Press Gang of
those days. He died in Holland, and was buried there. Both
these great-great-grandfathers, my father Algar Boswell
told me, apart from their many other trades of tin and cop-
persmiths, were good fist fighters, and used to fight on
travelling boxing-rings and booths.

My great-grandfather Tyso Boswell, who was slain by
lightning with his cousin, Edward Heron, at Tetford, near
Horncastle in Lincolnshire, on 5 August 1831, was there for
the August Horse Fair at Horncastle.

Tyso's wife, in her single days, was Sophia Herne or
Heron. Sophia's father was Richard or Dick Hearne. His
wife was called Bonny.

My great-grandfather Tyso and Sophia had a large family.
One of the daughters was called Maria, and she was the wife
of John Gray, the Gypsy fiddler who is spoken of by John
Clare the poet, who taught him to play the fiddle, for there
was a stopping place or camp for Gypsies in the years around
1915 near Helpston and Wansford. This spot was called Langley Bush, so it's plain to see now that John Gray (daughters
Dora and Alice) the fiddler, and his wife Maria, who was my
grandfather Wester's own sister, does connect with the Gypsy
families visited by John Clare the poet at Langley Bush.

Wester Boswell or Silvester

My grandfather was Wester, short for Silvester Boswell.
He married Florence Chilcott at Yarmouth. He was born at
Dover in the year 1811 in the army barracks, for it was here

that he got his schooling in the barracks schools, for Tyso
his father, was also in the Press Gang or Militia, for periods
of soldiering. Silvester died on 22 April 1890, aged 79 years

Florence, or Fluer, as she was called for short, was born at
Norwich in January 1820, and died at the age of forty-three
Buried in East Ham Cemetery, near London. The following
are the records of my grandfather, and his wife Florence and
family:

Byron – born at Benwick, near Doddington, Cambridge
shire, 1839. He was a good fiddle-player, and could have
been taught by John Gray. Left for Wales in his young
days.

McKensie – born on Ascot Racecourse on Derby day, 1842

Oscar – born at Bray, near Windsor, in the year 1844.

Bruce – born at Stisted, near Braintree, Essex, 1847.

Julia – born at Litherland, near Sefton, Liverpool, 1850.

Wallace – born at Sutton in Cambridgeshire, near Ely and
Chatteris.

Trafalgar – named after the battle of Trafalgar. Born a
Plaistow, Newton, Essex, in the year 1856.

Laura – born at Barrow, near Woodbridge, Suffolk, in the
year 1859. My father told me she died at the early age of four
years.

My father was the youngest son of Wester Boswell, who
spent many of his latter years with my father and mother
and I think through these years together, Wester gave my
father these Records, that were given to me by my father in
the many years he spent with me and my young family in
our talks together in our leisure hours.

I could mention dozens of places where my father
travelled to, just to show his children the places where his
father travelled in his young days, and I think it's been a
case of following in father's footsteps all along the line as I
see it. In those days of persecution, there were places and
districts that would be by-passed, and so these routes were
picked where they could move in comfort, and earn their
living without much trouble. These counties I have men
tioned, Norfolk, Suffolk, Essex, Cambridgeshire and Lin

colnshire, being sparsely populated in the past, and mostly agricultural, would be the most suitable for living off the 'fat of the land' as the saying goes, I mean rabbits, hares, game, and the birds, and the *hotchi* (the hedgehog). There was all this when I was a boy, although beginning to be restricted in many cases, but these counties must have been everything to my people in those days, with the many commons and open spaces available to them.

Wester, Tyso, and his Father Shadrack

The line of information I give here is that my line of descendants landed on the east coast of England, the south-east to be correct, in the 1750s. This information has been handed down from my great-great-grandfather, Shadrack Boswell, to his son Tyso Boswell, and from him to his son Wester Boswell, who, in his day, was known as Dictionary Wester Boswell, a man of good memory and education far in excess of any known Gypsy of his days, who was proud of his nationality, and because of his knowledge and learning, was sought after by some of the most prominent writers of the Gypsies in translating the Romany language into English, especially with authors like B. C. Smart, M. D. and H. T. Crofton, in their book, *The Dialect of the English Gypsies*. In my opinion, this is the only book that the authors openly give credit to my grandfather Wester Boswell for the assistance he gave them, quite truthfully, because he trusted them to the full, for at that time of his life, many of his people objected to him giving *gaujos* the idea of learning the Romany language as he knew it. I must say, that I'm very proud today that he was such a good judge of character, that he was right, in the end, to confide in them, because my father told me of many of the so-called Romany Ryes paid visits to him for information in those days, offering tobacco or smokes, by way of introduction, with very little success. I believe my grandfather Wester was intelligent enough to realize that his people before him had something original about them, that he was so interested in them that he probed into the past generations, evidently through his father Tyso and others of that day, and he then got as far as his grandfather Shadrack Boswell, and came to a full stop and here is where the south-east coast comes in, with the first families of the Boswells, Hearnes, or Herons, and some few Lees and Lovells in the first landings of these families The dates do go back to the 1750s or thereabouts, for my father Trafalgar Boswell has told me that Shadrack's family did not speak any English language, only Romany, until they eventually learnt it themselves. This record is now given to you as I have got it from my father. He, in turn, was a scholar too, and although his interest in his own people was great, he never brought his information to the front as he might have done, but he had a wonderful memory to his dying day, and at all times proud of his father and forefathers. He always wished me to put on record some of the things I have related here. I never realized it should have been done until he died in 1949, and then I made a start by writing something about my people of the past.

I am still of the opinion that my forefathers came from Egypt, and not India, and that information was handed down from my father to me, from his father Wester, how long it took them to get here, and what countries they travelled though, the course they took, I cannot tell, over the continents, travelling some six hundred years to land here.

The Family of my Father and Mother
Trafalgar and Athaliah were married on 11 October 1878 Father was twenty-two years old, and mother was eighteen years old. The profession on the Register is 'Horse Dealer' and father's address at that time was Borough Road Birkenhead. Grandfather Wester's profession was given as a cane worker. Mother's address on the Register was given as Brickfield Road, Everton. Her father James Whatnell was a horse dealer.

My Brothers and Sisters
First, Lewis and Leon, twins – born at Belfast, Ireland, 21 June 1879, were christened at St Ann's Church, Belfast.

Lewis, one twin, died when eight weeks old at Belfast, and was buried at Borough Cemetery, Belfast, Ireland.

Second twin Leon – died when nine weeks old, and was buried at Glassenova Cemetery, Dublin, Ireland.

Brother Nathan – born at Belfast, 12 September 1880. Christened at St Ann's Church, Belfast. Buried in Ingoldmells Churchyard, near Skegness.

Brother Bruce – born in Belfast, 24 November 1881. Christened at St Ann's Church. Belfast. Buried in Ingoldmells Churchyard, near Skegness.

Brother Arthur – born at Liverpool, 23 January 1883, and christened at St George's Church, Everton, Liverpool. He still lives in America, with one son, George. He married about 1916, a girl by the name of Boswell. Her grandparents was one of the Boswells transported.

Brother Eden – born 27 April 1885, at Inverness, North Scotland. He was named after Sir Robert Eden, Premier of Scotland, and christened at the Cathedral, Inverness. Died at Brough, near Hull, in 1952, and buried at Anelby Cemetery, near Hull.

Brother Gilbert – born 25 May 1887, at Liverpool. Christened at St Mary's Church, Walton, near Liverpool. Living with me.

Brother Josh – born 21 August 1889, at Blackpool. Christened South Shore Church.

Sister Laura – born on 5 November 1891, at Liverpool. Christened at St Mary's Church, Walton, Liverpool. Buried at Skegness Cemetery.

Sister Sarah Linda – born 23 March 1893. Christened South Shore Church, Blackpool. Died at Bournemouth.

Myself, Silvester Gordon – born 25 February 1895, at South Shore, Blackpool.*

Brother Lewis – born 23 June 1897, at South Shore, Blackpool. He died 2 February 1933. Buried at Skegness Cemetery.

Sister Ida, better known as Dixie – born 27 April 1899, at

* Gordon Boswell has followed the Gypsy tradition of large families: he has seven children and fifteen grandchildren.

South Shore, Blackpool. Died in Rauceby Hospital, October 1966. I buried her with Sister Linda in Bournemouth Cemetery.

Little brother, John Wesley. He was named after John Wesley Baker, the evangelist, and lived but seventeen days. Died 31 March 1905. Buried Eastwood Cemetery, near Southend, Essex.

My Mother and her Family

My mother was Athaliah Whatnell. He father was Jim Whatnell of Liverpool, and was a horse dealer in those days. He was in partnership for some years with my Uncle McKensie, my father's brother. They bought Irish horses for the Liverpool Tram & Bus Company. He was related to the Coopers in Essex on his mother's side. My mother's mother was called Adelaide Smith, her mother and father was old Frank Smith and his wife Hona, who died at the age of one hundred and two years. She and Frank were travelling the day she died. They had pulled on the side of the road to rest and have a meal. She had a smoke from her pipe, which she was never without, and told her children that she was not ill, but just worn out. She said her old bones were like a bit of old nettle stalk that she pulled out of a hedge beside her, and she then lay back and died. This is true, for my father and mother told it to me many times. Hona is buried in Leyton Cemetery, near Blackpool. My mother had a brother called Herbert, and two sisters – Alice died a young woman, and Ada married Nathan Lee, who travelled Scotland most of his time. Both died there. Some of their family are in Scotland today. Herbert's wife was Bertha. Her people lived mostly around Portobella near Edenborough. They had a son called Willie, who died a year ago last September, and the sisters were Alice and Dorothy, since died. The three girls now living, Bloater and Nunna (these are the nicknames they carry from children) and the other is called Talker. My grandmother Adelaide had two brothers, Adolphus Smith, who's wife was Sibey. They had a big family at Blackpool. The sons were Arthur, Frank, the girls were

Suby, Adie, and Tilly. Arthur was a sharp-tempered man, and would not stand any nonsense from anyone. This led him into trouble many times in his life. His wife was Lottie, old Noah and Goosey Young's daughter. Lottie was a good wife to Arthur, and they were, in my opinion, a happy pair. They had a daughter called Ivy. Then there was another brother of my grandmother, Walter Smith, with his wife Matilda, who was a Lamb, who lived the latter days of their lives at Lowestoft, a place called Kirtley Run, which I have mentioned here before, in these notes about this family.

Appendix II

Death of a Well-known English Gypsy

Sylvester Boswell (Westa'aros), famous for his deep Romanes,* died 22 April and was buried 24 April† in Blaybrick Hill Cemetery in the same tomb with his two sons Byron and Bruce. He died in Walton Workhouse where he had been placed by his family about four years ago when his mind began to fail. He was 79 years of age, but most of the Gypsies here believe him to be much older: his nephew, J. Gray, insisting that he was at least 100. Upon his giving up tent life his goods were divided among his surviving sons and relatives and, as his subsequent death did not actually occur in the camping ground, the usual Gypsy custom of destroying the deceased's effects was not in this case followed. He is, however, said to have himself made away with a number of small valuables before his retirement. I remember after that event took place, the ground underneath and around his small tent was dug up to a considerable depth in the hope of finding some of the articles which he is believed to have somewhere secreted.

– *Journal of the Gypsy Lore Society*. Old Series II, p. 191, January 1890. (Item A in *Notes and Queries* by John Sampson.)

* *Vide*: Smart and Crofton's *Dialect of the English Gypsies*; Groome's *In Gypsy Tents* and Morwood's *Our Gypsies in City, Van and Tent*.

† 1890.

Appendix III

Those who knew Sylvester Boswell personally or through the numerous references in Messrs Smart and Crofton's *Dialect of the English Gypsies* may be interested in a few extracts from his old notebooks now in the possession of a member of the family. The book is a small duodecimo with several leaves torn and missing. The writing throughout is laboriously neat and the orthography distinctly 'Westerious'. On the parchment cover is written:

> Register Book
> of famleys allso
> famaley Memerandum
> Book January 1841. 1847
> Redgister Book 1847

and a considerable portion of this small volume is filled with records of the births, marriages and deaths of his own family and members of the Smiths, Hernes and Chilcotts. These entries are characterized by his usual minuteness and quasi-legal precision of phrases, e.g. 'in or near a Barne', 'Dover in Kent', 'London, Essex' etc. etc. and the Christian era is religiously given in each case with ingenious variations: 'in the year of our Lord october the 13th 1839 on Sunday', 'first fryday in July the 5th in the year of our Lord 1850', 'June the 15th 1842'th year of our Lord' etc. etc.

A pathetic story records the death of his wife:

... this is the year the dear mother of this family flower or Florence died on Thursday morning half past 7 sep 8th 1864 and was buried on the 11th sep 1864 at East Ham Sussex. Died at North Woolwich and left 7 Dear Children to layment for her and her husband Byron Mackenzie Oscar Bruce Julia Wallis Trafalgar and Loriae the youngest Child.

Silvester Boswell her Husband that layments for her most bitterly his Dear flower, dear flower.

Part of the book is devoted to accounts kept in a rather primitive fashion:

Bought of Jarned a poney Cart	£7	10
and sold to Mr Smith of felexholm for	9	0
sold the Black mare that cost	3	15
to Ealey for	5	10
Bought the same poney again at	5	10
and sold again to Mr Simons at Barnett for	9	0

Another page gives us 'the Rode from Birmingham to Mach and the towls' and a similar entry concludes 'this distance cost 7s 8½d with one Horse and Cart and a loose Horse. But this is the nearest rode and the Best from Birmingham to Peterborough.'

Other entries seem to be the rough draft of a Will:

... allso I Desire the old Watch to be keeped in my own famley as long as there is one left and not to be parted with on aney account this was my fathers years Before he died and he and old hearn died in one second slayen By thunder and lightning and a fire Ball at tetford in Lincolnshire this tyso Boswell my farther Dyed and his Cusin August the 5th 1831.

I bought this fiddle at Colchester this is an old one allso. But the age I do not know But I brought September 1861 its a Emartis [Amatis] fiddle and a very valuable one I have say I Desire that they shall not go out of my Children care but be among these selves This I Crave of you Silvester Boswell.

This fiddle however passed into other hands.

– *Journal of the Gypsy Lore Society*. Old Series III, p. 24[8], April 1892. (Item B in *Notes and Queries* by John Sampson.)

Appendix IV

A TRAVELLING TRADERS' GUILD?

By R. A. R. Wade

A proposal of the greatest importance was publicly announced by Gordon Boswell at Appleby Fair this year. The fair itself, in the second year of its new venue, was a great success. Everyone had become more familiar with the new scheme and, without any significant exception, cooperated to make it work smoothly. The Council had laid on a water supply and other convenient amenities, including even a tractor and driver constantly standing by to assist any caravan which might get bogged down in wet weather. There was a general atmosphere of goodwill all round, and the Police and local authorities were completely satisfied with the good order which prevailed. In short it was triumphant proof of what can be achieved by calm and sensible negotiation between intelligent Gypsies and public authorities, the whole thing having been organized by Gordon Boswell and a small committee of helpers in consultation with the local councils and the Police. It clearly demonstrated that by similar peaceful and businesslike methods the Gypsies could help themselves on a wider national basis.

Since the 1965 census of Gypsies the Sociologist Research Section of the Ministry of Housing and Local Government have been engaged in a great deal of fieldwork and have compiled in draft a bulky Report,* full of humanity and common sense, which it has been my privilege to see and comment upon. Provided it is not shelved (a risk with all draft official reports), but shortly published as intended, it is certain to affect profoundly the public attitude towards the travelling community and promote a better understanding.

* *Gypsies and other Travellers* (H.M.S.O.).

It should also prompt definite action in the long-expected move to provide camps for them, with the result that the various public bodies concerned will be looking for a sensible, organized body, truly representative of all the country's Travellers, with whom they can consult, as they have done in the past with the Showmen's Guild, in consequence of which showmen are much better off for camping-places today than the Gypsies. Gordon proposes a similar organization for Travelling Traders and I here set out an extract from his inspiring address delivered from a loud-speaker van on Appleby Hill in June last.

I'm not an educated man, but I'm a man of experience and I do know the way these things are done. Some of us have been talking this over – the travelling people who are on this ground – and we say and agree that we are willing to form this Travelling Traders' Association (suppose that will be the name). You may not see results right away, in the first year ... But there's got to be a beginning to all things, and this would go – it's a great idea. Because you are driven from pillar to post, out of one district to another and you have no rest on the road. There is a remedy for our people; we are British subjects; we are entitled to Justice. Other minorities in this country, even those who come from abroad, are looked after and their human rights respected, but you've got nothing, nor nobody to care, nor no place to live, nor even to rest. You are technically a people 'of no fixed abode'. I have told the authorities and all concerned that you have the abodes, but you've nowhere to put them.

But you're doing nothing. I am an old man: I'm 73 years old. If it doesn't come in my day, it'll come in the time of some of you youngsters. And what I would like to see is some camps up and down the country. I'd like to see three types: a permanent camp where old people can go and stop and rest and be left in peace; a transit camp where you can come from one town to another and pay to go in and travel the country from the North to South if you wish; and camps where you can stop in decent comfortable conditions in the Winter months. I want to know if you are going to remain silent like we have done for all these years – like my grandfather, and great-grandfather who put his tent on this very hill in Appleby with packhorse and rods. We are in 1967 and with these facilities when we get them, I'm not thinking about you men. I'm thinking about your little children. The time has come when they should *all* be able to go to school and get some education. We all hear plenty in the news these days about education, new schools, bigger colleges, new universities, not one mention of the Romany, the Gypsy, the traveller, in regard to all this – and it's up to you to get it for your children too. They are the people I am concerned with. That's all I've got to say. The rest is up to you.

– *Journal of the Gypsy Lore Society*. Third Series, Vol. 47, pp. 29–31. January to April 1968.

Editor's Notes

Prologue

1. Literacy is still unusual among British Gypsies and other Travelling people, and itinerant children are probably receiving even less education than hitherto owing to the remorseless move-on policy of local authorities.

2. The legend of 'the fourth nail' is widely believed among European Gypsies. It is now known, from documentary as well as philological evidence, that the Gypsies came from northern India, and reached eastern Europe in the thirteenth and fourteenth centuries. Their language still has a strong Indian base although much added to by accretions from the lands through which the Gypsies have wandered. When they reached Europe the leaders of the Gypsy migration propagated the legend that they had been cursed by God for their part in forging (albeit unwittingly) the nails for the Cross and condemned to wander for seven hundred years, visiting the holy places of Christendom. Some of them had forged documents purporting to be from the Pope saying that they must be given charity and free passage in their wanderings, and that they came from a country called 'Little Egypt'. Hence they became called Egyptians, then Gypsies.

1 Childhood

3. The Gypsies have always adopted, nominally, the religion of the host country that they happen to be in; thus we have Shia Muslim Gypsies in Persia, Sunnis in Iraq, Orthodox Christians in Greece, Catholics in southern Europe and Anglicans in England. For the most part this religion is the thinnest of veneers, and the Gypsy is true to a set of animistic beliefs which he has brought with him. The *Beng* (Devil) is as real to him as God, and the Gypsy is much concerned with ghosts, or the spirits of the departed. Except in India all Gypsies believe fervently in the existence of one God. Gordon Boswell's parents were unusual in being quite genuinely converted to Nonconformist Christianity.

4. 'With the wheels run outside' means that the back wheels of

the wagon were too large to be accommodated under the body as they are in a lorry or dray. The back axle therefore had to be extended beyond the sides of the wagon. The front wheels, being required to turn, had of course to be smaller, and to be accommodated underneath the body on a turn-table to which the shafts were fixed.

The 'Gypsy caravan', or covered horse-drawn living wagon, so commonly associated with Gypsies, was in fact a short-lived phenomenon. Traditionally Gypsies lived in tents such as the one Gordon Boswell was born in (and they still do over most of eastern Europe and Asia), and Gordon's father's 'Tongs' wagon was probably one of the first. The *vardo* (Gypsy caravan) is now giving way very rapidly to the 'trailer caravan' pulled by a lorry or car, although there were over forty *vardos* at Appleby Fair last year (1969).

5. White is the colour of mourning, and therefore of ill-omen, among Gypsies as it is among most Indians. It is rare that they have white articles among their belongings: even sheets, if they have them, are likely to be coloured. Many Gypsies, apparently otherwise poor, will possess a wealth of expensive chinaware: Crown Derby being the favourite make.

6. *Gaujo* means non-Gypsy.

7. A *lorry* is a four-wheeled, flat spring-wagon pulled by a horse.

2 Boyhood

8. The European Gypsy has retained many Indian customs connected with ritual cleanliness. One of them is that if a dog (an unclean animal) licks the plate the owner will destroy the plate, even if it is Crown Derby worth five pounds, for it can never be made clean again by no matter how much washing and sterilizing. It is interesting that the horse is held to be perfectly clean, and a Gypsy will cheerfully eat off a plate that a horse has licked. We can almost discern a horse-fetishism among the Gypsies: even now when he lives in a modern house or trailer caravan a Gypsy will surround himself with the horse motif: he will have china horses in his cupboards, chrome-plated horses on the bonnet of his scrap lorry, a horse-shoe tie-pin, horseman-type boots and clothing. If he can possibly afford it he will keep a few horses in a field somewhere, although he has no real work for them to do. The horse, of course, has been his stock-in-trade,

mode of transport and constant friend for centuries of wanderings; but we can perhaps see a link with the horse-fetishism described in the early Hindu epics such as the Mahabharata and the Vedas.

9. *Fellies* are the components of the wooden part of the rim of the wheel.

10. Custom among Gypsies has changed here since the virtual passing of the horse for transport. In horse days it was usual for the women to go out and earn the money, and the men to stay around the camp. The reason for this was that it required the men to look after the horses and, if made necessary by police intervention, to harness them up and move on to another site. If they had to do this they would leave signs (*patrins*) on the roadsides to guide the women when the latter returned to the empty camp. The men could busy themselves in camp making the clothes pegs, baskets, and other artifacts for the women to sell.

Nowadays it is more usual to find the women at home or in the trailer caravan while the men are out, collecting scrap, macadamising driveways or tarring the roofs of barns. When there is seasonal farm work all the people will be out, for the women and children work beside the men in the fields, and the trailer caravan will be locked up.

11. By 'other classes of people' Gordon Boswell means people who are living the nomadic life but are not Gypsies, i.e. they have no, or little, Romany blood. They are looked down on by Gypsies. The common assertion of the vulgar: 'There aren't any real Gypsies left today are there?' is quite untrue: possibly there are more real Gypsies in this country today than there ever have been. Many live in houses and often disguise the fact that they are Gypsies, but in secret they are tremendously proud of their race. But there are many people with no Romany blood living in trailer caravans, including a growing number of Irish Tinkers, who are a race of their own, with their own language (Shelta) and who are finding it easier to get a living in England than in Ireland. But the travelling population was swollen in the last century by the army of itinerant labourers who built the canals and railways. A person living in a caravan is not necessarily a Gypsy. The true Gypsies have not out-married very much, and families like the Lees and the Boswells have kept themselves racially very pure. *Gaujo* blood has been brought in, though, by adoption of *Gaujo* children (see Note 13).

12. Esmeralda Lock was the eldest daughter of Noah Lock and

Delaia Jones (Welsh border Gypsies) and she was born in 1854. In 1870 she met Hubert Smith, the Town Clerk of Bridgnorth, who took her and her two brothers on a tour of Norway and wrote an account of the trip in *Tent Life in Norway*, which had Esmeralda as the heroine. In 1874 Smith married her, but she couldn't stick his sedentary life and ran away with Francis Hindes Groome, an author of several books about Gypsies including *In Gypsy Tents*. Groome took her to Germany and married her in Edinburgh in 1876. She was very popular in Bohemian circles, in London and elsewhere, and is depicted in several of Dante Gabriel Rosetti's pictures. Groome found life with her too hectic and asked her to leave him, which she did although she still loved him. In 1898 he divorced her and she returned to her own people. She was run down by a bus in 1939 and died at Rhyl, and is buried at St Thomas's church there.

She was a great friend of Doctor Dora Yates, the present Secretary of the Gypsy Lore Society, and the above information was extracted from Dr Yate's excellent book *My Gypsy Days*.

3 Travelling

13. This sort of anarchic social security is widespread among Gypsies, and it is most rare for a Gypsy child to go to an orphanage, or for an old Gypsy man or woman to go to a workhouse or 'home'. On being orphaned a Gypsy child is invariably taken into the family of relatives or friends, and such is the Gypsy's love of children that no Gypsy would refuse any child a home. Gypsies have only one feeling about 'family limitation' and that is the more the merrier. The persistent legend that Gypsies used to steal *Gaujo* children is probably without foundation, but in eastern Europe and in Asia they still act as a free orphanage service: a village girl who 'gets into trouble' and cannot rear her baby herself will give it to the Gypsies, knowing that it will be looked after by them as their own children and brought up as a good Gypsy. This practice was not unknown in England in the last century, and I know of one woman, now a contented wife and mother and very much a Gypsy, who was found by Gypsies wandering in the London streets after a bombing raid in the Second World War, and when, after a search, they failed to discover her parents they simply took her into their own family and brought her up as one of their own children.

14. Such is the xenophobia of a certain type of countryman

that in every village there seems to be *one* evilly disposed person who will telephone the police at the first appearance of a Traveller or Gypsy. The police then feel it incumbent on them to come and drive the Travellers on, and this constant harassment and persecution gets steadily worse as the years go by. I have had the experience of driving in a horse and cart through the southern counties of England and being followed for mile after mile by a police car, the occupants of which, thinking I was a Gypsy, wished to make sure that I did not stop for a moment in the area they were responsible for. I have seen horses pulling *vardos* with their necks raw from the collar, owing to the fact that their owners have been so remorselessly hounded by the police.

15. The Gypsy looks upon all possessions as stock-in-trade: he will 'have a deal' with anything except his children and his wife. He loves to 'chop and change' – the very word *chop* here comes from Romany and means to swap or exchange. If you offer a proper Romany man the right price he will sell you anything: his caravan, his crockery, his horse, his dog or his gun (in spite of what Gordon Boswell says about a good lurcher dog being held invaluable and not to be sold at any price. There is always a price). The Gypsy's often repeated assertion: 'I wouldn't part with that for all the money in the world guv'nor – I'd sooner sell me old Mother!' or: 'I wouldn't sell that for a thousand pounds!' simply means that he wants a higher bid. The Gypsy despises the man who is not willing to 'have a deal'.

16. British Gypsies do *not* roll hedgehogs in clay to cook them.

5 The Boy becomes a Man

17. About seventy-eight miles.

18. The 'step dance' is one of the few surviving English country dances, and is still practised extensively by Gypsies all over the country. Like many 'folk arts' it has survived among the Gypsies when it has died out, practically, among the settled population. Even nowadays every Gypsy encampment will produce from at least one trailer caravan a board specially carried to dance on. It will be flung down beside the fire outside at night and people will take turns 'stepping' on it. The steps of the dance are very fast and intricate, but the dancer stands more or less in one place: as Gordon Boswell says 'he was all in one position'. Often another person of the opposite sex will leap up and

confront the dancer and dance with him or her step for step – neither touching the other but holding their arms straight down by their sides.

The music will be provided by a melodion, a mouth organ, or by 'tuning', which is what Gypsies call 'mouth music', and at which many of them are very good. Or even by rattling a pair of spoons and beating on a box or a tin tray.

Another folk art which survives among the Gypsies is the folk song. Many Gypsies, young as well as old, know scores of songs going back to Elizabethan times. The Gypsy, being generally illiterate, has an amazing memory (*vide* Gordon Boswell's total recall of the names of whole large families of long-dead people who were camped on such or such a common sixty years ago. Although Gordon Boswell is not illiterate he is no bookworm and is used to having to commit things to his memory). The Gypsy remembers songs right through – the latest 'pop number' that he has heard on a juke-box as well as the oldest ballad or folk song. From the great mass of new songs that come out every year he will remember one or two that particularly appeal to his taste, and these will probably be added for ever to the Gypsy repertoire, and handed down from generation to generation.

19. Among the other relics of Indian Vedic ritual cleanliness among British Gypsies is a strong aversion to washing clothes, or even hands and faces, in any receptacle used for washing, eating, utensils. Every true Gypsy family, no matter how poor, will have two washing basins: one for hands and one for crockery, and if a cup – even a Crown Derby one – is washed up in the wrong one it will be smashed or otherwise disposed of. It is for ever *mochaday* – ritually unclean, and no amount of washing can abate the impurity. This is strikingly in accordance with Indian tradition.

Gordon Boswell and his wife, Mabel, still adhere rigidly to these customs in their clean modern bungalow.

20. The Romany language is a complete and highly inflected language, with a Sanscrit or Hindi base and accretions from the language through which its speakers have passed. There are still Gypsies in Britain (contrary to general belief) who can speak the complete language with no English or Welsh words in it, and most Gypsies know enough words (albeit with no grammar) to carry on a conversation that the uninstructed *Gaujo* cannot understand. Gypsies are very secretive about their language, and many of them will not admit to knowing a word of it until they

know you very well. In continental Europe and all over the Americas 'deep' inflected *Romanes*, in its several distinct dialects, is still widely understood and spoken.

21. *Tatting* means rag collecting. The *tatter* will try to *mong* (beg) his rags or other scrap if he can, but if he can't will pay for them.

22. *Mush* means man.

6 *The Soldier*

23. *Pal* is a word that English has borrowed from Romany, and it does not have the slightly coy overtones for the Gypsy that it has for the *Gaujo*. It really means brother.

7 *Blighty*

24. *Crown and Anchor*. One of the only two gambling games permitted in the British Army by Queen's Regulations. 'House' is the other – civilianized as 'Bingo'. A man with a Crown and Anchor Board can make a nice bit of money, if he keeps his wits about him.

25. As explained in Note 5, white is the colour of mourning for both Gypsies and Indians and has very sinister connotations for them.

8 *Up North*

26. *Stir* is short for *stirbaen* – prison.

27. *Kushti* means good.

9 *The Horse Trade*

28. By this Gordon Boswell means that he would turn them out on some good pasture where the ponies would graze and rest and recover from their journey from Russia. They would then look 'brand new', i.e. in good condition.

29. An *accommodation* is a wagon or cart (four- or two-wheeled vehicle) with a hooped tent on it that can be lifted off and set on the ground. When travelling the owner and his family live under the tent on the vehicle, but when camping for some time they put the tent on the ground so that the vehicle can be used for hawking or other work. There was at least one at Appleby Fair last year (1969).

30. A *lurcher* is a dog of carefully mixed descent the aim of the breeder being to produce a dog with the speed of a greyhound but with a rough coat and more intelligence. A pure-bred greyhound will very seldom catch a hare by himself a good lurcher will, because he uses his head as well as his legs. Greyhounds, Scots deerhounds, Irish wolf-hounds and sheepdogs have all been used in the production of lurchers. A good one is highly prized. He should be silent (a lurcher should never bark), and be trained to go into a field and bring back a hare or pheasant or other game to his owner. I have known a Gypsy who trained his lurcher to go straight back to the camp on the command 'Come here!' and most lurchers are trained to make themselves scarce when a stranger comes along. Gypsies still bet on their lurchers' performance, and anything goes in boasting of the prowess of one's dog.

31. Elopement is still occasionally practised as a marriage custom among British Gypsies: the couple disappearing for a few weeks and then coming back, the girl no longer a virgin, to be first scolded and then welcomed by the girl's parents whereupon a properly (and often lavishly) solemnized marriage takes place. Among continental Gypsies abduction, supposedly by force often takes place, the groom bodily carrying his bride away and the girl's parents *pretending* to be annoyed even though they are not. Bride purchase is also common among other Continental Gypsies (notably the Kalderash tribe), a hollowed-out loaf of bread being placed in the tent or caravan of the girl's parents, and the man's father, and other relatives, putting money in it. Jumping over a broom plant used to be the only ceremony needed by British Gypsies to solemnize a marriage (the broom being a symbol of fertility), and it is still sometimes practised even when the marriage is also solemnized in church. Most Gypsy marriages last a lifetime: divorce, desertion and adultery being practically unknown among Gypsy people. The fact that the Gypsy husband takes his family with him wherever he goes, and almost never spends a night away from his wife (some never do at all) may account somewhat for the extraordinary stability of Gypsy marriages.

11 *Scrap*

32. From the time they left India, Gypsies have been famous for their knowledge of metal working. Even today much blacksmith work, tinkering, repairing of copper vessels and other

metal skills are done exclusively by Gypsies in many parts of Europe and Asia. The itinerant worker has the advantage that when he has done all such work in one district he can move on to another. Thus the Gypsy in Britain turned naturally to scrap metal collection when other trades failed him, and most of them now earn at least a part of their living from this activity. Without their services this country would rapidly be smothered in its own scrap, and the little untidiness that is inevitable around the camp of a scrap collector is nothing compared to the universal mess there would be if no scrap was collected.

Very small Gypsy children will classify correctly any metal.

33. Gordon Boswell has a long narrow strip of land between a straight road and a drain on the dead flat fen about a mile out of Spalding. He calls it 'The Ranch Scrapyard'. He lives in a comfortable modern bungalow, kept scrupulously clean by Mabel his wife and a lady who comes in to help. There is a bungalow next door inhabited by one of his sons and his family, and generally several trailer caravans belonging to other children of his, or to friends. Most of the land is taken up by an enormous pile of scrapped cars and other scrapped material. He owns, or rents, various parcels of land scattered about the countryside, and on these he keeps a large number of horses, ponies and donkeys. Mr Boswell's house, and yard, are the headquarters of an extensive web of Gypsy activity and enterprise and there are always people coming and going: as in all Gypsy purlieus there is a constant air of drama and excitement.

12 *What Gypsy means*

34. Appleby Fair, for long an important horse fair, has in very recent years become the most important meeting place for Gypsy people from all over Britain. It is rapidly achieving the same position among British Gypsies as *Les Saintes-Maries-de-la-Mer* among French and Spanish and Italian ones. It is the one place where, every year, British Gypsies can be sure of meeting friends and relations, where marriages are made, and where the national or racial consciousness of this people can be renewed. The Fair was threatened with closure in 1965 by the local councils, but a deputation led by Gordon Boswell persuaded them to change their minds. Gordon Boswell now presides over the Fair and organizes it, and has made it a model of good, spontaneous, almost anarchic (in the best sense of the word) administration. In

1969 there were seven hundred trailer caravans on the Fair Hill (and many more camped illegally on the road) and over forty horse-drawn caravans. Hundreds of horses changed hands, many thousands of people flooded the little town of Appleby, and the police asserted afterwards that no crime was committed and they were given no trouble whatever.

35. A *yog* is a stick fire.
36. A *grai* is a horse.

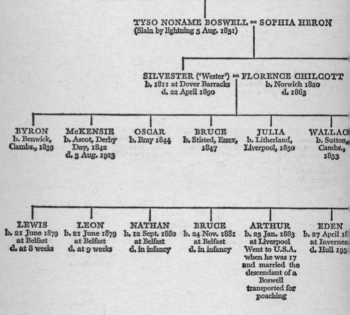

SHADRACK BOSWELL = CINDERELLA WOOD

TYSO NONAME BOSWELL = SOPHIA HERON
(Slain by lightning 5 Aug. 1831)

SILVESTER ('Wester') = FLORENCE CHILCOTT
b. 1811 at Dover Barracks   b. Norwich 1820
d. 22 April 1890   d. 1863

BYRON	McKENSIE	OSCAR	BRUCE	JULIA	WALLAC
b. Benwick, Cambs., 1839	b. Ascot, Derby Day, 1842 d. 3 Aug. 1923	b. Bray 1844	b. Stisted, Essex, 1847	b. Litherland, Liverpool, 1850	b. Sutton, Cambs., 1853

LEWIS	LEON	NATHAN	BRUCE	ARTHUR	EDEN
b. 21 June 1879 at Belfast d. at 8 weeks	b. 21 June 1879 at Belfast d. at 9 weeks	b. 12 Sept. 1880 at Belfast d. in infancy	b. 24 Nov. 1881 at Belfast d. in infancy	b. 23 Jan. 1883 at Liverpool Went to U.S.A. when he was 17 and married the descendant of a Boswell transported for poaching	b. 27 April 18 at Inverness d. Hull 195

Family Tree

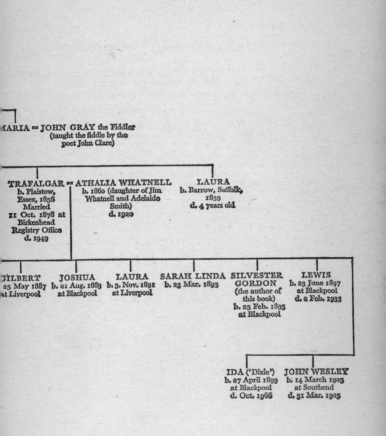

MARIA = JOHN GRAY the Fiddler
(taught the fiddle by the
poet John Clare)

TRAFALGAR = ATHALIA WHATNELL
b. Plaistow,
Essex, 1856
Married
11 Oct. 1878 at
Birkenhead
Registry Office
d. 1949

b. 1860 (daughter of Jim
Whatnell and Adelaide
Smith)
d. 1920

LAURA
b. Barrow, Suffolk,
1859
d. 4 years old

GILBERT
25 May 1887
at Liverpool

JOSHUA
b. 21 Aug. 1889
at Blackpool

LAURA
b. 5. Nov. 1891
at Liverpool

SARAH LINDA
b. 23 Mar. 1893

SILVESTER
GORDON
(the author of
this book)
b. 25 Feb. 1895
at Blackpool

LEWIS
b. 23 June 1897
at Blackpool
d. 2 Feb. 1933

IDA ('Dixie')
b. 27 April 1899
at Blackpool
d. Oct. 1966

JOHN WESLEY
b. 14 March 1905
at Southend
d. 31 Mar. 1905

PENGUINEWS *AND*
PENGUINS IN PRINT

Every month we issue an illustrated magazine, *Penguinews*. It's a lively guide to all the latest Penguins, Pelicans and Puffins, and always contains an article on a major Penguin author, plus other features of contemporary interest.

Penguinews is supplemented by *Penguins in Print*, a complete list of all the available Penguin titles – there are now over four thousand!

The cost is no more than the postage; so why not write for a free copy of this month's *Penguinews*? And if you'd like both publications sent for a year, just send us a cheque or a postal order for 30p (if you live in the United Kingdom) or 60p (if you live elsewhere), and we'll put you on our mailing list.

Dept EP, Penguin Books Ltd,
Harmondsworth, Middlesex

Note: *Penguinews* and *Penguins in Print*
are not available in the U.S.A. or Canada